The Earned Value Management Maturity Model®

▲

The Earned Value Management Maturity Model®

Ray W. Stratton, PMP, EVP

𝄃𝄃𝄃
MANAGEMENTCONCEPTS

⦅⦅ MANAGEMENTCONCEPTS

8230 Leesburg Pike, Suite 800
Vienna, VA 22182
(703) 790-9595
Fax: (703) 790-1371
www.managementconcepts.com

Printed in the United States of America

Library of Congress Cataloging-in-Publication Data

Stratton, Ray W., 1946-
   The earned value management maturity model / Ray W. Stratton.
     p. cm.
   Includes bibliographical references and index.
   ISBN 1-56726-180-9 (pbk.)
     1. Project management. 2. Cost control. I. Title.

HD69.P75S77 2006
658.15′52—dc22   2006046234

▲

About the Author

Mr. Ray W. Stratton, PMP, EVP, has been involved in earned value management for over 25 years. His earned value management experience began as a control account manager for the software development of a real-time military communication system. He is founder and president of Management Technologies (www.mgmt-technologies.com), which has been providing program management training and consulting services for over ten years. His Earned Value Experience™ workshop has been taught to over 1,000 participants. He is a Project Management Institute (PMI®) certified Project Management Professional (PMP), and AACEI (Association for Advancement of Cost Estimating, International) certified Earned Value Professional (EVP). Mr. Stratton sits on the PMI® College of Performance Management Governing Board as Vice President, Research and Standards. He is also a member of the Defense Acquisition University Alumni Association (DAUAA). He is Chair of the Computer Science Industry Advisory Council at California State Polytechnic University and a member of the Editorial Board for *Projects@Work* magazine.

Mr. Stratton retired from the Naval Air Reserve at the rank of Captain. He last commanded an engineering unit that supported a variety of studies and projects on behalf of the Naval Air Systems Command, laboratories, and ranges. He holds a masters and a bachelors degree in electronic engineering from California State Polytechnic University, Pomona. Ray can be reached at raystratton@mgmt-technologies.com.

▲

Dedication

This book is dedicated to John Moseley (1945–2005). John was my team leader when I worked as a software engineer on my first project at Hughes Aircraft Company. It was 1977. John decided to leave the defense industry in pursuit of his dream of operating his own business. As he was leaving, he recommended to management that I take over as the team leader of the 12-person software development team. Thus began my journey down the path of project management that has resulted in this book and experience I have tried to share with you. If you find some useful ideas and knowledge in this book it is due, in part, to John's faith in me to lead his team onward while he followed his dream.

We remained best friends until the end.

▲

Table of Contents

▲

Preface

Do you have an earned value management system in place? Do you need to have an earned value management system in place? Are you thinking about adding earned value management to your project management controls? The Earned Value Management Maturity Model® (EVM³®) will lead you from a simple earned value management implementation, to one that meets earned value management standards, to one that operates very effectively at minimal cost. No matter whether you have used earned value management for years or are just trying to get started, this book can help you get to the next step in earned value management implementation. It shows you how to create a scaleable earned value management system that can evolve to meet earned value management system standards and government-directed earned value management implementations.

Whether you need to address the ANSI/EIA 748 standard or just improve the data coming from your earned value management system, the Earned Value Management Maturity Model will help you get where you want to be. This book will also help you to decide if earned value management is the right tool for your project or organization to use to monitor cost and schedule performance.

Earned value management has been a project management best practice for over 30 years. It is the best tool to monitor project cost and schedule performance. Yet it remains a relatively unused practice in most industries and projects. This book will show you how you can implement earned value management very simply and very quickly. It will also show you how to add robustness and accuracy to an existing earned value management system to get increasingly better cost and schedule data for project management decision-making. Finally, it will show you how to optimize your earned value management system.

The U.S. ANSI/EIA Standard 748 defines 32 guidelines for earned value management. Do you need to meet all 32 guidelines to perform earned value management? The answer is "No."

The Earned Value Management Maturity Model will show you which of the 32 guidelines you must meet to perform basic earned value management. As your organization moves up the maturity model, you satisfy additional guidelines. At Level 3 you are compliant with ANSI/EIA 748, but you can go much further. EVM^3 Level 4 and EVM^3 Level 5 guide you toward optimizing the value of the earned value management system so that project managers receive the most timely and the best cost and schedule information at minimal cost.

This book has two parts. Each part is independent of the other. Part I discusses earned value management concepts, principles, terms, and analysis tools. If you are not familiar with earned value management this part of the book will give you the theory of earned value management, its terms, and its analysis products. Part I also contains the first textbook discussion of *Earned Schedule*. If you are not familiar with the new Earned Schedule parameter, you should at least read Chapter 2. Part II presents the Earned Value Management Maturity Model. Part II covers the five levels of the maturity model and what is expected at each level of capability.

Until the last decade, most of the knowledge of earned value management was contained within the U.S. Department of Defense (DoD) project management directives, policies, and contracts. Until the mid 1990s any books about earned value management focused on the DoD formal implementation and its related complexity. This very formal earned value management implementation was justified by the taxpayers' investment in cost reimbursable contracts worth billions of dollars. Prior to about

1995, most textbooks described what appeared to be a complex, multidimensional, expensive, and bureaucratic way of managing projects. Unfortunately, any potential user who read one of these books looking for a new project management tool would be discouraged from applying earned value management.

Late in the 1990s, more industries, companies, and nations began to see the value of earned value management. A few books were published that provided simplified explanations of earned value management. One key document that helped the spread of earned value management was the ANSI/EIA 748, "Earned Value Management Systems." This document brought into the public domain the concept of earned value management as used by DoD. However, the 32 guidelines in the ANSI/EIA 748 standard still required a significant investment in training and processes. Unless the project was very large or the organization had previously practiced earned value management as a DoD contractor, why would anyone want to use earned value management?

The Earned Value Management Maturity Model helps make it possible to scale the implementation of earned value management for any size project, from a small team project to a multi-billion dollar program. Once you have earned value management data, and cost and schedule forecasts for your project outcome, you are back in control. You know where your project is headed.

Ray Stratton, PMP, EVP
Brea, California

▲

Foreword

By Carl Pritchard, PMP, EVP

AN EARNED VALUE MANAGEMENT CULTURE

Are you mature? Professionally, of course. That's a much
tougher question than it appears to be on the surface,
and it's even more difficult to answer under the micro-
scope of a single area of professional practice. With the empha-
sis on earned value management systems being brought to bear
by the Office of Management and Budget's *Circular A-11* and
the admonitions for due diligence of the Sarbanes-Oxley Act,
the pressure has never been greater to prove that organizations
and individuals are professionally mature and are managing
their businesses (and more specifically, their projects) well.

Any attempts to draw conclusions about good management in-
herently bring with them some measure of subjectivity. Earned
value management, however, has long been about making the
case that the subjective and amorphous world of projects can be
objectively and rigidly reined in. That's no mean feat. In today's
world of "faster, better, stronger," it's difficult to serve the masters of both efficiency and accountability.

Enter earned value management. Organizations that apply earned
value management hold out for the promise of a clear means of
determining a project's progress, effective use of resources, and
potential conclusion. And that *is* the promise of earned value
management. But that promise can be thwarted by an inconsis-
tent application or a poor understanding of how earned value
management is actually implemented. Indeed, any organization
undertaking earned value management as a practice needs to

assess its capability for EVM implementation. Such capabilities rest in the hands of individuals, and as such, the protocols for implementation need to be made as clear as is humanly possible. There is a normal progression for the development of such protocols—individual then division then organization.

The individual experience with earned value management is normally somewhat stilted. There are data elements that are readily available to most projects and some that are not. In some organizations, the individual work packages may be clearly defined and outlined, but the resource costs may not be available. Or the resource cost information may be on hand, but the actual costs of the work performed may not be at the disposal of the project manager or the team. As such, individuals almost always must "make do" with whatever data are available to them. That's not an optimal environment for earned value management, but it can serve as a practical training ground for beginning to understand the mechanics of implementation. In many instances, it's times like these that make individuals aware of what they do not know. And knowing what we don't know can open the door for a thirst to learn how we can implement the remainder.

When enough practitioners in a single group determine that earned value management implementation is a necessity, there is a notable shift in culture in that group. Because there are multiple users, the data elements that support earned value management need to become consistent. This is a major change for many organizations, in that the way in which work is packaged, the way in which costs are captured, and the ways in which resources are applied to projects must become progressively more consistent. What a wonderful time for an organization. The pioneers who led the charge on earned value management get to see their vision come to fruition. Other participants are now playing along, and the rules of engagement are more clearly established.

This can also be a difficult time in the world of earned value management. With more players, earned value management becomes more visible, and thus also becomes a potential target. The administrative overhead associated with earned value management is challenged, as is the visibility of cost and pricing information in organizations without a history of open-book management. This time of growth is life or death for earned value management, as the practice will ultimately come under the gaze of senior management, meaning that senior management must endorse or subvert it. Endorsement comes with a host of benefits, including information tracking, forecasting, and reporting capabilities that some organizations only dream of. But endorsement also means the commitment of significant administrative resources and the willingness to become an "enforcer" as the need arises. Those latter roles do not sit well with some senior managers, and may sound the death knell for mature earned value management implementation. For those who can withstand the slings and arrows of earned value management critics, survival in this difficult developmental period can mean a future rich with an understanding of where projects are and where they're going.

With the advent of OMB *Circular A-11*, Section 300, the civilian agencies of the U.S. federal government took a major leap forward in terms of organizational maturity in earned value management. By setting clear guidelines of when earned value management systems must be applied and how the information they generate will be used, the government opened the door for consistent application and enforcement of effective earned value management practice. While such "on-high" edicts bode well for those who support the practice of earned value management, they do not guarantee success. They simply create the opportunity for those who want earned value management practice to thrive to succeed. True organizational success arrives with the application of clear standards (such as ANSI/EIA-748-A-1998) and the respect for those standards by the individuals responsible for supporting them. And that takes time. The culture shift to move to an effective earned value management system means a long-term commitment to a vision of improved understanding of incremental and global progress on projects.

While the government can force such commitment by edict, public and private organizations should work to win such commitment by illustrating the value of the practice and the promise that it holds. In the pages that follow, Ray's work should be read in two contexts—first as an informational treatise on the mechanics of implementation, but second as a cultural guideline. If, between the lines of the pages that follow, you can find the elements that map to your organization's culture, you can take first steps toward earned value management maturity. If you find affirmation that most of your practices already map to the ANSI/EIA standard, you should look for any areas where your culture can be improved (and you can use it as a wonderful "I-told-you-so" moment). In either case, look at the insights herein as a road map. For the beginner, it's a chance to see where the path leads and how you might traverse it. For the skilled professional in an organization with a rich EVMS history, it's clear affirmation that the process is evolving in the right direction.

Carl Pritchard is the Principal of Pritchard Management Associates. He is an Earned Value Professional as certified by the Association for the Advancement of Cost Engineering and a Project Management Professional as certified by the Project Management Institute. He is the U.S. correspondent for Project Manager Today (UK) *and is a member of the board of directors of ProjectConnections.com. He lectures, presents, and conducts research in the field of project management. His personal website is www.carlpritchard.com His e-mail is carl@carlpritchard.com*

▼

PART I

Earned Value
Management Basics

▼

CHAPTER 1

Introduction to Earned Value Management

Implementing any new process involves cultural change, emotional and financial investment, and acceptance of new ways of doing the familiar. So, why are more and more organizations opting to endure these difficult transitions to implement earned value management? Simply stated, over 30 years of experience demonstrate that earned value management is one of the most effective means available to monitor project cost and schedule performance.

Today's projects operate in an environment of overcommitted resources, demanding stakeholders, and changing technologies. Corporate fiduciary responsibilities are increasing, and CEOs and CFOs must forecast earnings that may be dependent on both their internal projects and customers' projects. The current status of projects, their likely completion date, and their final cost are crucial data items that CEOs and CFOs must possess. Earned value management provides a powerful tool for obtaining these data.

Earned value management is applied toward the end of the project planning effort and is dependent on good project plans. Because it is a way of instrumenting a project for monitoring cost and schedule during project execution and control, it quickly reveals poor project planning or the inability to execute a good plan. During project execution and control, earned value management provides insight into the project's current cost and schedule status, helping the project manager balance the triple constraints of cost, schedule, and requirements.

Three metrics form the basis for earned value management (they are explained in more detail later in this chapter). At any point in the project, these three metrics reveal:

- The project work that should have been completed

- The work actually completed

- The cost of completing that work

It may appear that earned value management adds little to the traditional concepts of project monitoring. Any project manager should know what is to be delivered, what has been delivered, and how much has been spent delivering it. However, the power of earned value management is its ability to shift the point of view from deliverables planned, deliverables completed, and funds spent to the *value* of work planned, the *value* of work done, and the funds spent. This transformation to an all-economic basis allows analysis that is otherwise not possible.

To understand the limitations of traditional project metrics, consider the common practice of monitoring projects using a schedule (or a list of met and unmet milestones) and a financial report. The schedule (Figure 1-1) reveals the activities started, completed, underway, early or late in starting, and early or late in being completed. The schedule provides a general sense of current project status by comparing where each activity stands relative to its planned status. However, the schedule does not differentiate between types of activities: some are small efforts and some are large efforts, some are on the critical path and some are not. The schedule may be able to provide a qualitative sense of the project being ahead or behind schedule, but quantifying the schedule condition is difficult or impossible.

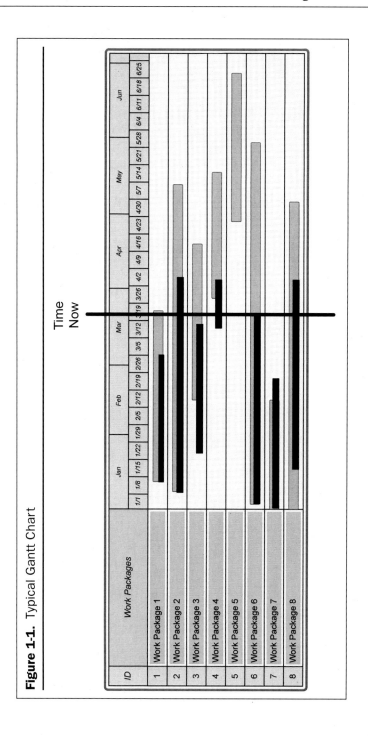

Figure 1-1. Typical Gantt Chart

You might look at a list of milestones (Figure 1-2) or deliverables and compare the planned completion dates with the current status. Here you have even less information than you did when looking at the schedule. Some milestones were supposed to be met at this point and some milestones have been met. Some milestones may have actual dates different from the planned dates, other milestones may have a best guess completion date different from the planned completion date. Using a list of milestones, you might obtain some qualitative insight into the project's progress, but you don't have enough quantitative information for any depth of analysis.

Figure 1-2. List of Milestones

Milestone	Original Plan	Current Plan	Actual Date
Milestone A	1/15/06	1/15/06	1/20/06
Milestone B	5/14/06	5/15/06	5/30/06
Milestone C	8/23/06	9/2/06	
Milestone D	3/23/07	4/20/07	
Milestone E	5/15/07	5/15/07	
Milestone F	10/28/07	12/28/07	
Milestone G	12/6/07	12/6/07	

The project financial report (Figure 1-3) reveals how much of the total project budget has been spent. However, it cannot provide answers to such questions as: "Were the funds spent well?" or "Was any work completed?" Without such information it is impossible to know whether the project budget will ultimately be underrun or overrun. All that is known is that money has been spent on the project.

Earned value management quantifies project progress and compares actual progress to planned progress and funds spent. It does so using three metrics: Planned Value (value of work planned to be completed), Earned Value (value of work actually completed), and Actual Cost (funds spent). These parameters are determined for each project time period, and also cumulatively from project inception. While some suggest that earned value management is difficult, it really only adds one element to traditional project management—Earned Value.

Figure 1-3. Summary Financial Report

Budget Item	Expenses to Date	Remaining Funds	Project Budget
Labor	$356,778	$2,509,066	$2,865,844
Material	$347,896	$506,560	$854,456
Subcontractor	$578,621	$405,652	$984,273
Travel	$79,425	($20,471)	$58,954
Overhead	$24,361	$30,284	$54,645
Project Totals	$1,387,081	$3,431,091	$4,818,172

Earned value management provides information that is useful to all levels of management. The project manager can use earned value management data to help manage the project. Team leaders can use these data to help manage their teams. Program managers and project portfolio managers can use earned value management data collected across all their projects to help identify poor project performance, reallocate resources, reset priorities, and terminate efforts that are likely to fall short of return-on-investment expectations. Chief project officers and CFOs can forecast project expenditures and completion dates, allowing better predictions of corporate revenues, expenditures, and profits. The CFO can employ these forecasts to develop financial statements detailing next year's projected corporate financial outlooks. Moreover, earned value management data can provide data for reports required under the Sarbanes-Oxley Act of 2002.[1]

Whether the industry is information technology, new product development, aerospace, pharmaceuticals, construction, or any other, earned value management provides valuable project insight for any project stakeholder, from the team leader to a corporate stockholder.

Earned Value Management

- Provides useful information for all levels of management
- Is applied to projects at the end of the planning cycle
- Requires good project planning
- Provides instrumentation for monitoring cost and schedule performance
- Helps balance the triple constraints of cost, schedule, and quality
- Provides the value of work completed
- Can estimate project completion date and final cost
- Assists in developing forecasts of corporate financials for project-based businesses

---

NOTE

1. The Sarbanes-Oxley Act of 2002 is a U.S. government regulation that increases the responsibility of corporate CEOs and CFOs to accurately report their companies' financial condition and financial outlook. It requires that "financial statements and disclosures fairly present, in all material respects, the operations and financial condition of the issuer." For a corporation whose primary revenue is from the completion of projects, earned value management data should be a key component in development of these forecasts.

CHAPTER 2

Basic Concepts of Earned Value Management

Percentage spent is not percentage done! Does this statement surprise you? Many projects exceed their budget yet still fail to deliver the promised outcome. If percentage spent was percentage complete, when 100% of the project budget is spent the project would be done and everyone would be happy. Most project managers know firsthand this is rarely the case. Percentage spent simply makes a statement about financial expenditures; it is not an indicator of project progress.

The same holds true for time. Spending time on a project does not mean the work is being accomplished at an appropriate pace, or even that the right work is getting done. It just means that the clock on the wall has moved forward.

Schedules can provide some insight as to progress, as can deliveries or completed milestones. But is the completed work worth what was spent to get it done?

Earned value management asks you to think about what has been accomplished *without* thinking about how much has been spent or how much schedule time has been consumed. Understanding this concept, and using it in estimating the work completed, is the major cultural impediment to using earned value management correctly.

PLANNED VALUE: THE PLANNED VALUE OF WORK

The most fundamental concept of earned value is that work is worth the planned or negotiated value (budget) of the work. Depending on the industry, this value might be set by a formal contract, an annual budget, or a price to be paid for the end product. This concept flows down into the project as teams, subcontractors, and vendors agree to provide certain goods or services for a set budget or contract. Earned value uses the budget as the metric to answer the question "How much work do you have to do?" In earned value management terminology, *scope* is synonymous with *budget*.

A $10 million budget means that the sponsor (customer, stakeholder, resource provider, etc.) agrees that the project results are valued at $10 million. Otherwise, the two parties would have agreed on a different value. The value simultaneously represents two separate concepts: (1) the expectation of spending $10 million and (2) the work is worth $10 million. (The inclusion of contingency funds in earned value management will be discussed later.)

For example, consider building a custom home. You ask an architect to design a home worth $500,000. The architect looks at the local housing market and develops blueprints for a home worth $500,000. You select a contractor to build the home and upon completion you receive a bill for $600,000. You pay the bill, reluctantly, consoling yourself with the thought that you now own a $600,000 home. It comes as a surprise when the local real estate broker exclaims, "You have a nice half-million dollar home." The value of the work is not what you pay for it; it is what you agreed it's worth at the start.

Planned Value is the earned value management term for the value of work. The Planned Value is the value of all project activities. While it might sound like the project budget, it really is the sum of each activity's time-phased budget, created by associating the applicable budget to each detailed work activity and the work schedule. Thus, each piece of work has two attributes: its value (allocated budget) and its planned completion date (allocated time, or schedule). The sum of the Planned Value for all project activities should equal the total project budget, less any funds set aside for risk management or not yet allocated to a specific activity. Today's powerful scheduling tools, resource pools, and planning make it easy to determine the Planned Value. It is simply the cost of resources to be applied to activities over their time frame.

For example if an activity is planned for four months, and is expected to use one person in month one and two people for the remaining three months, the Planned Value for the activity is the cost of seven staff-months. Further, the expectation is to spend one staff-month in month one and two staff-months in each of the final three months. When we use the term *time-phased budget* we are indicating what we expect to spend each month based on the work *planned* to be completed that month and the cost of the *planned* resources.

Plotting the cumulative value of all project activities and their budgets on the *y*-axis with time on the *x*-axis reveals a cumulative Planned Value going from zero to the total value of the project. The total Planned Value for a project is also termed the *Budget at Complete,* or *BAC.* This is the value of all work in the project plan and thus also represents the scope, in financial terms, of the project. The plot will not be a straight line because it reflects the value of activities and products to be completed each period (month). This curve, called the Performance Management Baseline (PMB), is the cumulative Planned Value of all the products and services that should be accomplished each period. In Figure 2-1, the cumulative value is $15 million. The PMB captures both the value and time frame of all project work. It is the reference line against which monthly project performance is measured.

The PMB can be viewed as a conversion of project funds to project deliverables, internal products, and support tasks. At the start of the project we have all our funds and no work has

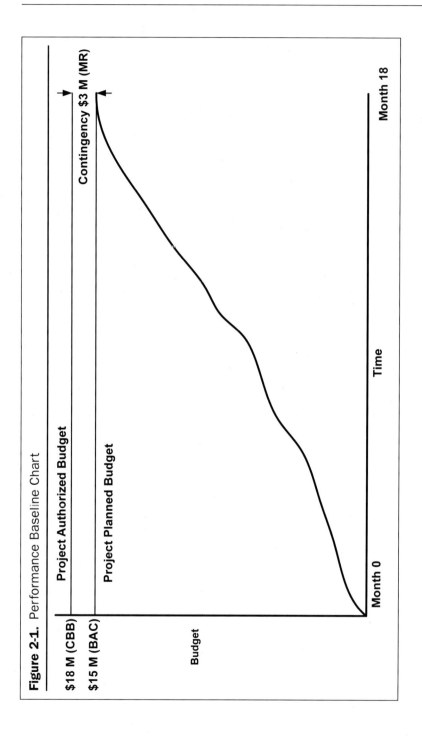

Figure 2-1. Performance Baseline Chart

been completed, so the Planned Value is zero. At project's end we have spent our funds and all the work is done, so the Earned Value equals the Planned Value, which equals budget at complete (BAC). The project's schedule performance will determine *when* the Earned Value line meets the BAC.

The PMB is relatively easy to create when a project is properly planned using contemporary project planning and scheduling software. If the project's activities are properly linked and scheduled, and resources with expected costs are assigned to each activity, the expected cost of resources for each activity sets the value of the activity. Summing the value of all the activities to be completed each month and then adding that sum to all the previous months' Planned Values yields the cumulative Planned Value. Plotting the cumulative Planned Value on the *y*-axis over time on the *x*-axis provides the PMB. The final cumulative Planned Value at the end of the project is the total value for all the activities from the start of the project to the end; this is the project's BAC. The BAC might not be the contract or project value—instead, it is the expected cost of all the resources needed to complete the planned work. Depending on the nature of the project this value might be an internal budget for the project or the cost to a customer for a cost-reimbursable contract.

The BAC should be ultimately derived from a bottoms-up estimate of all project works. However, the estimate might be performed to determine a bid amount in a competitive environment. Profit and contingency might be added to the bid amount. Once the project is awarded and negotiated, the final BAC may be less than estimated. This amount is then distributed to the project activities. So, in either case the amount may be less than the estimate for the proposal, but it is still a valid Planned Value for the work since the contract value was determined by the marketplace. This is the value and cost that should not be exceeded if the profit and cost to the customer are to be met.

When a financial reserve or profit has been set aside, we have two distinct budget amounts:

- The contract budget, which is an amount agreed to by buyer and seller or sponsor and project manager. It is called the contract budget base (CBB).

- The project manager's plan, which sets aside some funds for contingencies, profits, or other categories. In earned value management parlance, the remaining amount of funds is the BAC.

The project plan expects to consume all the BAC, but hopes not to use contingency or profit funds to complete the work. The BAC is the term of most interest in earned value management. Earned value management uses the term *management reserve* (MR) for contingency. Figure 2-1 shows that there is a $3 million contingency in the project. An overall expenditure of $18 million is authorized, but plans call for only $15 million to be spent.

EARNED VALUE: THE VALUE OF COMPLETED WORK

Earned Value accrues as a result of completing activities. It is a parameter unique to earned value management. Completion of each activity contributes to the project's Earned Value. At project beginning, the total Earned Value is zero. As the project progresses, completion of each activity adds to the project's total Earned Value. When lengthy activities are underway, objective, or if necessary subjective, measurement methods provide partial Earned Value until the total activity is complete. At the end of the project, the total Earned Value equals the cumulative Planned Value (recall this is the value of the BAC) because all the scheduled work is done.

Note that this discussion does not mention actual costs or funds spent. A key element of earned value is that work has value equal to its budget, not what was spent completing the work. *We do not need to know how much was spent or how long we have worked on an activity to determine its Earned Value.*

Once the value of completed work is known, it can be plotted on the Performance Management Baseline (Figure 2-2). Comparing the Planned Value to the Earned Value reveals whether the planned work is being completed at a sufficient rate. In Figure 2-2, at this specific point in the project Planned Value was forecast to be $8 million, but the Earned Value (value of all the work that can currently be claimed as completed) is only $4 million.

ACTUAL COST: THE COST OF COMPLETING WORK

The third parameter of earned value is Actual Cost. It is exactly what its name suggests. It is the cost of completing each activity, often reported in project financial reports using a Work Breakdown Structure (WBS). Comparing Actual Cost to Earned Value indicates whether the project expenditures were correct for the amount of work completed. The ability to perform this comparison is one of the key benefits of earned value management: the capability to compare the *cost* of the work completed with the *value* of the work completed.

Traditional project management techniques use a spend plan and costs to date (Figure 2-3) to ascertain whether spending is occurring at the correct *rate*. When the project is below the spend plan, management will ask, "Are we on schedule?" "Will we underrun the project budget?" "Are there too few people on the project?" When the project is above the spend plan, management will ask, "Do we have too many people on the project?" "Are we having problems?" "Will we overrun the budget?"

These questions are all excellent ones. Yet, mere comparison of the actual costs to the spend plan doesn't allow anyone—not even the project manager—to answer them. Management might try to infer information about progress, staffing levels, and future expenditures, but the actual data yield no useful insight. When the *value* of the work completed is added, the first question to ask is, "Have we spent more or less than the value of the completed work?" Based on the answer to that question, it is

Figure 2-2. Performance Baseline Chart with Earned Value

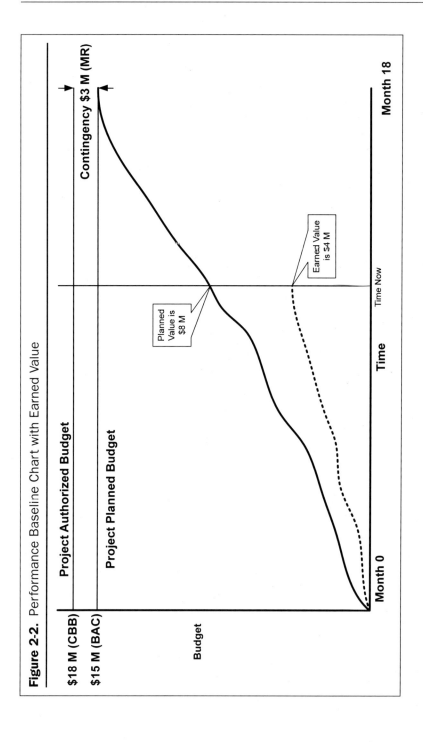

Figure 2-3. Spend Plan versus Funds Spent

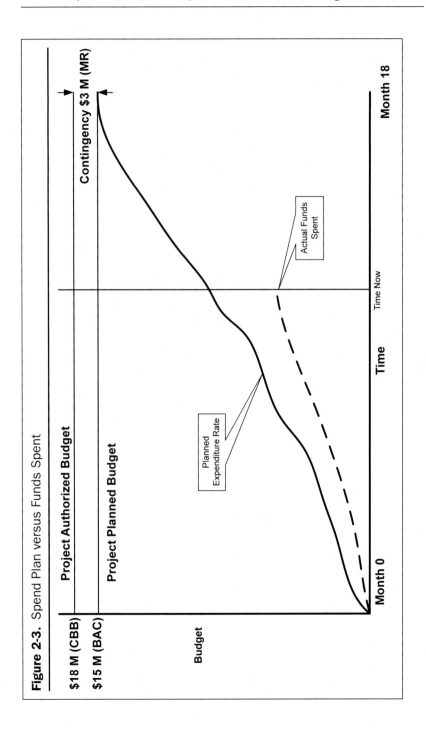

possible to look further into the project to determine the "why" and forecast the project's final outcome.

An Example: Relating Planned Value, Earned Value, and Actual Cost

A project manager goes to the systems engineering department to request specification development. The project manager describes the nature of the system and the customer's requirements. Systems engineering tells the project manager it will cost $40,000 to write the specification; the project manager expected this cost to be $25,000. Systems engineering then expresses concerns over getting good requirements and the impact of slow customer reviews. The project manager attempts to allay these fears by assuring systems engineering personnel they will receive requirements that meet their expectations prior to startup and by personally assuming the risk of slow customer reviews.

Subsequent negotiations yield a price of $32,000 to write the specification. This cost is the Planned Value, as it reflects the agreement that the value of the specification is $32,000. Months later, systems engineering delivers the specification. So, the Earned Value is equal to the Planned Value: $32,000. However, the associated financial report reflects expenditure of $37,000 to write the specification. The Actual Cost is $37,000. Expended costs do not make the specification worth $37,000; the budget was exceeded for some reason. If systems engineering spent only $27,000 writing the report, the specification would still be worth $32,000, as the value of a product is set at the outset.

THE CONTROL ACCOUNT CONCEPT

One of the key concepts of an earned value management system is the *control account*, previously known as a cost account.

The control account is found within both the project's hierarchical WBS and OBS structure. In fact, it is the one element in each structure, other than the whole project, that is common to both and thus links the two together. As the name suggests, this is the point in the WBS or OBS where control is exercised. It follows the sound project management rule that those closer to the work should be the ones to monitor individual work assignments, estimate progress, address technical details, perform tactical risk management, and be accountable for quality, cost, and schedule performance for their products.

In the WBS (see Figure 2-4) the work scope is decomposed into manageable chunks that can be assigned to a specific project team leader, organizational element, or subcontractor. Within the WBS only one manager or team leader is held accountable for completing this work. This person is the *control account manager* (CAM). (If the work scope falls into two or more teams' responsibilities, the WBS must be taken one level deeper to subdivide the work to satisfy the this rule.) In the OBS (Figure 2-5) the project organization is decomposed into departmental func-

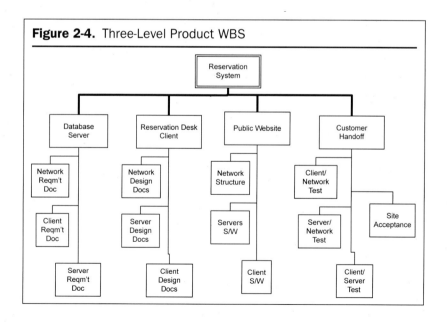

Figure 2-4. Three-Level Product WBS

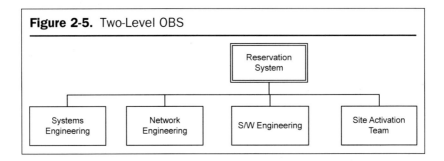

Figure 2-5. Two-Level OBS

tions, integrated product or project teams, subcontractors, and other support structures. The OBS is largely influenced by the project manager's organizational preferences and the nature of the company's general use of functional, matrix, or project structures.

The control account is where detail planning occurs and the resulting plan produces a Performance Management Baseline for the control account. The control account is also the intersection of the OBS with the WBS (Figure 2-6). Summing the planning of all control accounts through the hierarchy of the WBS or OBS produces the identical overall project Performance Management Baseline.

A Performance Management Baseline may also be determined for each of the intermediate levels in both the OBS and WBS. There is no requirement for the same number of levels in each structure, so comparing WBS level 3 to OBS Level 3 may produce different Performance Management Baselines.

Since each control account has a Performance Management Baseline, it follows that during project execution both cost and schedule information must be collected so that the performance of each can be compared to the control account's Performance Management Baseline. So, finally, we have arrived at the point where the organization's financial cost collection system and scheduling system plays into the WBS structure. If control account costs are to be reported to the control account manager

Figure 2-6. Cost Accounts

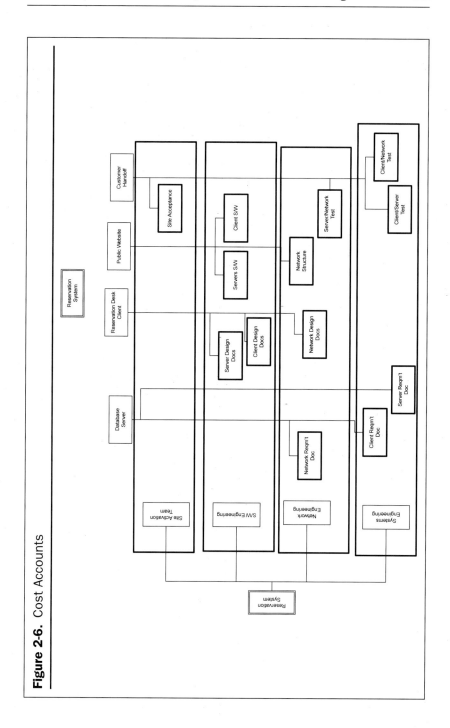

(CAM), the financial system must provide that detail. Lacking that, staff hours spent may be used with some loss of earned value management thoroughness (and EVM[3] maturity level). Likewise, the scheduling system should provide schedule information to the CAM for the tasks within the control account. The cost and schedule information provides Planned Value, Earned Value, and Actual Cost at the control account so that earned value management analysis can be done at this level within the OBS and WBS.

Because a formal earned value management system requires that basic earned value management data be collected at the control account, and summed through both the OBS and WBS structures, it is usually necessary to embed both structures into the project cost and schedule data collection systems. This can be a challenge for accounting and scheduling systems that do not provide a means to show both structures within their account numbering scheme. So, while a goal might be a detailed control account structure, the limiting factor may be the existing financial or scheduling systems. One cannot perform schedule analysis without schedule information, and one cannot perform cost analysis without cost information. Often financial and scheduling system limitations determine the number of possible levels in OBS and WBS the size (work scope) of the project control accounts.

FUNDS, BUDGETS, CONTINGENCY, PROFIT, OVERHEAD, MANAGEMENT RESERVE, AND UNDISTRIBUTED BUDGET

Earned value management gives some very specific meanings to words we generally use very casually.

Funds is a term that does not appear in earned value management. Generally we associate the term with the amount of money set aside for the project as part of an annual budget cycle or funding authorization. It may be more or less than the budget needed to complete the project, or might be part of a fiscal year funds allocation as part of a multi-year project. Funds pay bills and payroll through the accounting system. *Funds* is synonymous with *money.*

Management Reserve (MR) is a formal earned value management term and refers to money held at the project manager level to address risk and cost issues that may arise during project execution. When MR exists, formal control of MR is required to show when it is used and what control accounts receive the funds. When control accounts complete work under budget, the unused money is deposited in MR. Think of MR as a checking account for unknown unknowns. It may be the same as a contingency, depending on the organization's use of the term *contingency.* Since MR is not assigned to a control account it is not part of the Performance Management Baseline or BAC.

Profit is not an earned value management term. Profit is money that the organization hopes to receive if the project completes on cost. If MR is not consumed it adds to profit, but if consumed, the target profit should still be the result of the project.

Budget, in earned value management terms, is generally the same as Budget at Complete (BAC). This is the amount of money that is expected to be spent performing the scheduled work. Because it is based on the scheduled work, it is usually the Planned Value of all the work shown on the project schedule and Performance Management Baseline. It may be less than the funding, and the difference might be contingency.

Overhead is a tax on project expenditures to pay for the organization's infrastructure. This may include salaries of senior management, pooled project support centers (labs, quality services, document control, etc.), lighting, desks, floor space, and phones. In earned value management it is important to anticipate, record, and control overhead costs to the project. When projects have negative cost variances it should be possible to determine if project direct costs or overhead (indirect) costs, or a combination, caused the cost variance. Generally the project can only be accountable for direct costs. The ANSI/EIA 748 standard requires that indirect cost managers be identified so that they can be accountable for indirect cost impacts to projects.

Undistributed budget (UB) is an earned value management term for money in the BAC that has not been allocated to a control account. The money may be due to recent contract scope and funding changes that have not been assimilated into the WBS and OBS, or the money may be for far-term work whose work authorization to a CAM has not been completed.

To summarize: All control account budgets plus undistributed budget equals the BAC and the cumulative Planned Value. It includes overhead costs (taxes) we expect to pay even though we might question if we are getting our share of these corporate services.

BAC plus MR is the maximum we hope to spend on the project and is likely the funds we have been authorized to spend. MR is our contingency for poor estimates of work effort required, risk, and other cost impacts. If there is MR left at the end of the project we can take it to the bank.

Profit is the difference between our cost and the customer's price. It might be zero or less if our cost exceeds our BAC and MR.

ANALYTICAL PRODUCTS FROM EARNED VALUE MANAGEMENT

Earned value management provides powerful tools to analyze project performance. With simply four parameters, Planned Value, Earned Value, Actual Cost, and BAC, it is possible to compute and plot a variety of metrics that provide insight as to how a project is doing and how it is likely to end.

Cost Variance and Schedule Variance

Cost and schedule variances can be determined using three basic earned value management parameters: Planned Value (PV), Earned Value (EV), and Actual Cost (AC). The completed work has an economic value (dollars or staff-hours of Earned Value), and that value can be compared with the value of Actual Cost and Planned Value. Subtracting Actual Cost from Earned Value allows cost variance (CV) to be calculated.

$$CV = EV - AC \qquad \text{(Formula 1)}$$

Note that the arrangement of the terms results in a negative cost variance when an overrun occurs (i.e., when Actual Cost is greater than Earned Value). Conversely, if expenditures are less than the value of the completed work (i.e., Actual Cost is less than Earned Value), there is a positive cost variance, or an underrun condition. Figure 2-7 illustrates cost variance graphically. The cost variance formula enables you to speak in terms of dollars or staff-hours above or below budget, or overruns or underruns. It is important to understand how these statements are much more meaningful with earned value management. Without earned value management, the comparison would be between what was spent and the financial spend plan and discussions would focus on being underspent or overspent.

Looking at the data in Figure 2-7, the Earned Value is $4 million and the Actual Cost is $5 million. Thus, CV is –$1 million (i.e., $4 million minus $5 million). A very important point is that during the organization's planning, it expected to complete $8 million of work and to spend $8 million. Without using earned value management principles, it might see an Actual Cost of $5 million and assume the project is *underspent*. However, using earned value management, the organization can determine that the Earned Value of the completed work is only $4 million. Thus, the project is not underspent, but rather overspent by $1 million! Therein lies the power of earned value management:

Figure 2-7. Illustration of Cost Variance and Schedule Variance

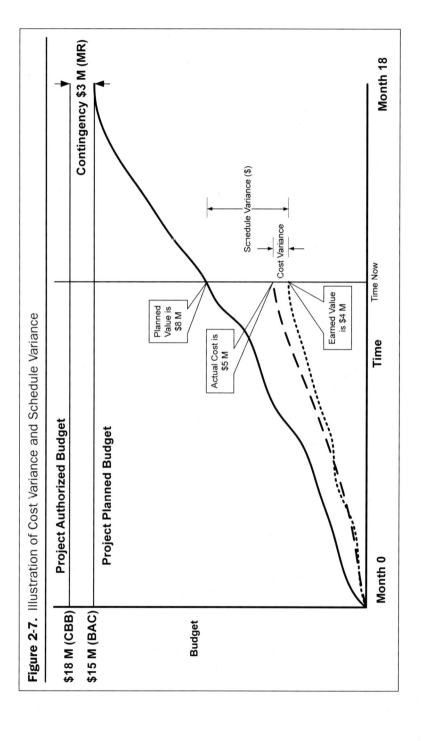

you can compare what you spent with what you accomplished, not what you spent with what you planned to spend.

It is possible to discuss schedule variance in economic units (staff-hours, dollars) using the vertical Performance Management Baseline axis or in time units (days, weeks, months) using the horizontal axis. Using the vertical axis is the traditional schedule variance approach and this method is universally understood by earned value management practitioners. Using the horizontal axis is a relatively new concept that is just beginning to gain acceptance within the earned value management community. In the discussion that follows, $ or t will be used as subscripts to distinguish schedule variance on the vertical axis ($) from schedule variance on the horizontal axis (t).

When referring to schedule variance (SV) computed from staff-hours or dollars, the term $SV_\$$ will be used. Subtracting Planned Value from Earned Value yields schedule variance.

$$SV_\$ = EV - PV \qquad \text{(Formula 2)}$$

Note that the arrangement of the terms results in a negative schedule variance if a project is behind schedule (i.e., if Planned Value is greater than Earned Value). Conversely, if more project work was completed than planned (i.e., if Earned Value is greater than Planned Value), then a positive schedule variance occurs. Using this formula allows project assessment in terms of being dollars or staff-hours ahead of or behind schedule. As in the case of cost variance above, both cost and schedule can be discussed in economic terms: dollars or staff-hours of variance. However, this type of schedule variance does not immediately convey whether the schedule variance is 1 week, 1 month, or more in units of time.

Using the data from Figure 2-7, Earned Value is $4 million and Planned Value is $8 million, so $SV_\$$ equals –$4 million (i.e., $4 million minus $8 million). In this case, inquiries regarding whether the project is on schedule would be answered with a nontraditional response: "No, it is behind schedule by $4 million." This is not an intuitive way to answer a question about (schedule) time. Most people would expect an answer like, "No, the project is behind schedule by three months." Our $4 million schedule variance means that there is $4 million of work that should be complete at this time, but is not.

Only people familiar with earned value management concepts would understand that a project could be behind schedule by a dollar amount. The concept of Earned Schedule allows schedule questions to be answered with more intuitive responses, ones that can be understood without knowledge of earned value management. (*Note: Earned Schedule* is both a new earned value management term and a title for a new concept in earned value data analysis.)

To understand schedule variance in units of time, you can look at the Performance Management Baseline and determine the point in time where the Planned Value equals the current Earned Value (Figure 2-8). Dropping a line down to the time axis allows you to see when the current Earned Value appears on the Planned Value line, enabling a statement about being days, weeks, or months ahead of or behind schedule. The term unique to this point on the time axis is *Earned Schedule*. (Lipke[1] developed the earned schedule technique.[2] Henderson[3] retroactively applied the concept to six completed information technology projects and found it to be of value. Vandevoorde and Vanhoucke[4] presented a comprehensive overview of earned value and earned schedule based metrics to forecast the project duration. Subsequently, Vanhoucke and Vandevoorde[5] performed research on 3,100 simulated project networks of varying topology and complexity and statistically validated the Earned Schedule concept and analysis products.) Rather than just looking at schedule performance using the value of work, earned schedule also looks at *when the work was to be completed*. It is the amount of "schedule time" the project has "earned" by completing work.

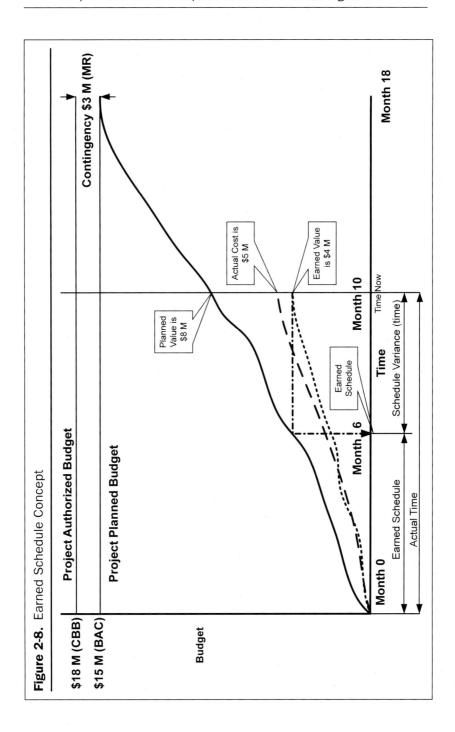

Figure 2-8. Earned Schedule Concept

Another new term obtained from the horizontal axis is the Actual Time, the time that has expired since project initiation. You can compute schedule variance on the time axis (SV_t) using Earned Schedule (ES) and Actual Time (AT).

$$SV_t = ES - AT \qquad \text{(Formula 3)}$$

This formula subtracts the actual amount of time spent on the project from the amount of schedule time earned by the completion of work. So, if the amount of work completed should have been done in month 6, but it is now month 10, the SV_t is 6 minus 10, or –4 months. The project is 4 months behind schedule (Figure 2-8). SV_t reflects schedule variance computed from Earned Schedule and Actual Time.

Cost and Schedule Percent Variances

Now you know that cost and schedule variances can be computed by calculating the differences in Actual Cost from Earned Value, Planned Value from Earned Value, and Actual Time from Earned Schedule, respectively. These are quantified amounts of the variance. However, the question arises: Is it a large or small variance considering the amount of work that was to be done? Cost and schedule percent variances answer this question. These concepts reveal the percentages by which the project is ahead, behind, overspent, or underspent *at this point in the project.*

The percent cost variance (CV%) is computed as follows:

$$CV\% = \frac{CV}{EV} \times 100 \qquad \text{(Formula 4)}$$

Note that this is a percent variance from the *current* value of Earned Value, not the BAC. So, while there might be a CV% of +10%, this finding only conveys that the costs are 10% less than planned for the amount of work accomplished. It is not the same as saying the project is or will complete 10% under budget.

The formula for computing the budget-based schedule variance percentage (SV%$_\$$) is

$$SV\%_\$ = \frac{SV_\$}{PV} \times 100 \qquad \text{(Formula 5)}$$

Like CV%, SV%$_\$$ is based on the *current* value of Planned Value, not the project completion date. An SV%$_\$$ of –15% only means that 15% of the work planned to be accomplished at this time has not been completed.

The time-based percent schedule variance (SV%$_t$) uses Earned Schedule values because they relate to the time axis of the Performance Management Baseline. Its formula is:

$$SV\%_t = \frac{SV_t}{ES} \times 100 \qquad \text{(Formula 6)}$$

Suppose the SV%$_t$ is +10% when the project has been underway 18 months (AT = 18). The work completed to date was planned to be completed about month 20 (18 x 1.10 = 19.8), and we are ahead of schedule.

Schedule Performance Index and Cost Performance Index

The most common artifacts of an earned value management system are the cost performance index (CPI) and the schedule performance index (SPI). While any reasonably good means of tracking project performance will produce some form of cost and schedule variance, the use of SPI and CPI as project metrics is unique to earned value management. These indices represent unitless measures of a project's performance efficiency. There is only one form of CPI but, as with the SV$_\$$ and SV$_t$, there are two forms of SPI: SPI$_\$$ and SPI$_t$.

CPI simply reveals the efficiency with which the project is using funds or staff-hours. To obtain CPI, divide Earned Value by Actual Cost.

$$CPI = \frac{EV}{AC} \qquad \text{(Formula 7)}$$

Since this formula divides two terms with the same unit of measurement, the result is unitless. Thus, the cost performance of two projects can be compared regardless of whether the CPI calculation uses dollars or staff-hours. Referring again to Figure 2-7, the CPI is only 0.8 (i.e., 4/5). Thus, at this point in time only $4 of work is being done for every $5 spent. A CPI of greater than 1.0 shows an underrun condition, and CPIs less than 1.0 show an overrun.

CPI can be plotted in a variety of formats. Figure 2-9 illustrates the most popular plot.

SPI can be computed in two ways: the traditional $SPI_\$$ and SPI_t using earned value schedule data. Both forms express how efficiently the project is using time; hence, both indexes use the term *schedule* in their name.

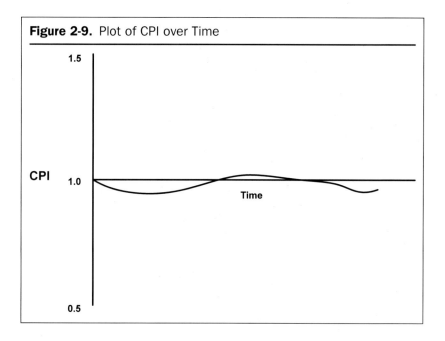

Figure 2-9. Plot of CPI over Time

SPI$_\$$ uses the traditional earned value management terms Planned Value and Earned Value, per the following formula:

$$SPI_\$ = \frac{EV}{PV}$$ (Formula 8)

Like the formula for CPI, this equation calls for the division of two terms having the same unit of measurement; thus, the result is unitless. Values > 1.0 mean ahead of schedule; values < 1.0 mean behind schedule. Referring again to Figure 2-7, the SPI is 0.5 (i.e., 4/8). Thus, at this point in time only half the work planned has been completed. An SPI$_\$$ less than 1 is not good; however, SPI$_\$$ does not reveal whether it represents behind-schedule condition of a week, a month, or a year. So, while SPI$_\$$ helps convey how well the time given to complete the project is being used, it fails to communicate exactly how far ahead or behind schedule the project is in terms of time.

As part of project portfolio management, it is tempting to compare the SPI$_\$$ values of two projects. Doing so is a common and serious mistake. Recall that at the end of the project the cumulative Earned Value must equal the cumulative Planned Value, which at this point also equals the BAC. Thus, the SPI$_\$$ must be 1.0 at the end of the project regardless of how early or late the project completes. Without knowing how much of the project is done, it is impossible to know if the SPI$_\$$ is still reliable or not. SPI$_\$$ does not have the analytical quality of the CPI, which remains valid throughout the project. At some time beyond the halfway point, the SPI$_\$$ of all projects tends toward its final value of 1.0, rendering it less and less useful as the project proceeds.

An SPI$_t$ computed from earned schedule data retains accuracy to the project's end. The following formula allows computation of SPI$_t$ using the Earned Schedule and Actual Time parameters:

$$SPI_t = \frac{ES}{AT}$$ (Formula 9)

Here, as previously, a value greater than 1 indicates an ahead-of-schedule condition. Referring to Figure 2-8, an Earned Schedule of 6 months and an Actual Time of 10 months equals an SPI$_t$

of 0.6 (6/10). Because 6 months of project work has been completed in 10 months, the SPI_t is less than 1. One might say that the project has been using time with only 60% efficiency for the first 10 months.

SPI_t is an improvement over $SPI_\$$, because SPI_t:

- Remains useful over the life of the project

- Allows side-by-side project comparisons

- Can be retained (like CPI) as part of the project historical files

Also, because SPI_t is accurate throughout the project, it also can be used to estimate the project's final completion date.

Both SPI_t and $SPI_\$$ can be plotted in a variety of formats. The most common is SPI versus time (Figure 2-10). This figure dramatically

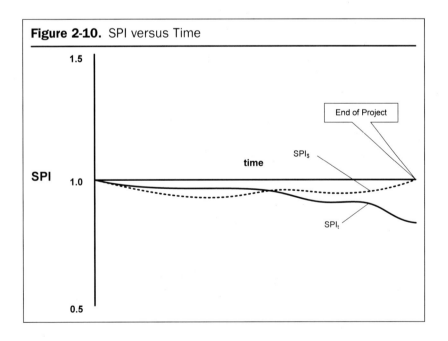

Figure 2-10. SPI versus Time

illustrates the fidelity of SPI_t compared to traditional $SPI_\$$ as the project completes. Since both SPI and CPI values vary in relation to 1.0, they are often plotted on the same curve to instantly convey the project's current cost and schedule performance, the history, and a projection of where these values might go next. This is powerful information that can be quickly and visually conveyed to customers, stakeholders, and senior management.

An organization that uses earned value management to perform analysis of the project performance using schedule and cost variances and SPI and CPI gains significant information about how the project is progressing. However, if the organization fails to use these data to extrapolate the project's final cost and completion date, it will have missed the most valuable payoff that earned value management provides.

Estimate at Complete

Thanks to CPI and SPI_t, and a budget that represents all the work to be done (BAC), all the parameters needed to predict the future based on the past exist. CPI conveys how efficiently money is being used, and SPI_t relates how efficiently time is being used. Thus, it is possible to predict when the project will be done and how much will be spent getting there. Of course, any extrapolation based on historical project data assumes that future performance will approximate past performance. There is common knowledge—and statistical evidence—showing this assumption to be valid for almost all projects. The project work is as difficult as it is. The work scope, whether understood at the outset or not, is what it is. The workforce skills, availability, and motivation are what they are. Unless there is a valid reason why the future will be different from the past, earned value management can be used to predict the final outcome based on past performance.

The project's estimate at complete (EAC), or final cost, can be derived using a number of formulas. One of the most common is shown below.

$$EAC = AC + \frac{BAC - EV}{CPI}$$ (Formula 10)

This formula starts with how much has been spent (AC) on the project, then adds the remaining work divided by cost efficiency. The numerator (BAC – EV) simply computes the remaining work. If the BAC is $10 million, and the project has earned $6 million, then the project still has to earn $4 million. The assumption is that it will do so at a cost based on the cost efficiency to date or CPI. This formula can be algebraically simplified as follows:

$$EAC = \frac{BAC}{CPI}$$ (Formula 11)

Dividing the project budget (BAC) by the CPI provides an estimate of the project's EAC, or final cost. Research and a review of hundreds of projects that have used earned value management have shown that the result of this calculation is the *most optimistic* estimate of final project cost. This is because past cost overruns are usually unrecoverable and future problems and risks may still materialize on the project.

Until the concept of Earned Schedule was introduced a few years ago, it was impossible to accurately estimate a project's completion date using earned value data. Recall that the traditional $SPI_\$$ is not a reliable indicator of schedule performance because $SPI_\$$ approaches 1 toward the end of the project and thus cannot be used to predict the project's end date. However, SPI_t is useful over the project's life and gives a useful parameter for estimating the completion date. There is a new earned value management term associated with earned schedule techniques that is analogous to the financial term BAC: Planned Duration (PD). PD is simply the expected duration of the project. Adding PD to a project start date yields the planned Project Completion Date (PCD).

Using PD, we can calculate Estimated Duration (ED), which is computed using SPI_t in a formula similar to the EAC formula.

$$ED = \frac{PD}{SPI_t} \qquad \text{(Formula 12)}$$

Adding ED to the project start date provides the Estimated Completion Date (ECD). Figure 2-11 depicts a comprehensive example of earned value management and the previously discussed terms and variances.

Percent Spent and Percent Complete

The following formula allows computation of Percent Spent (PS):

$$PS = \frac{AC}{BAC} \times 100 \qquad \text{(Formula 13)}$$

Similarly, Percent Complete (PC) is calculated as follows:

$$PC = \frac{EV}{BAC} \times 100 \qquad \text{(Formula 14)}$$

Of course, Percent Complete should be close to Percent Spent; however, if the two are identical, or nearly so (and also have a corresponding CPI of 1.0), then the project staff may be estimating the amount of work done by how much has been spent. This practice violates the concept of Earned Value being independent of Actual Cost. Practitioners expect CPI to be close to 1.0, but are suspect if it is 1.0.

As a final note on CPI and PC, research[6,7] involving hundreds of large U.S. Department of Defense programs indicates that once a project is beyond about 18% complete, the final CPI will not differ by more than 10% and will likely go down, not up.

Figure 2-11. Comprehensive Example

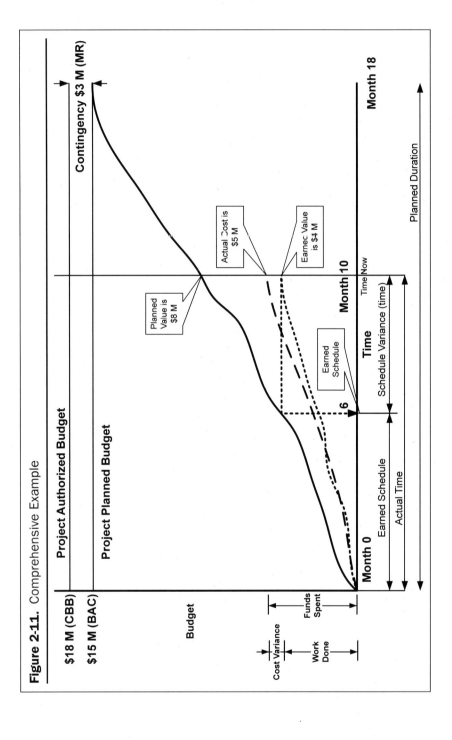

HOW EARNED VALUE MANAGEMENT SUPPORTS DECISION-MAKING

As any project portfolio manager knows, deciding on the relative merits of projects is challenging. An ever-changing landscape of user needs, customers, market pressures, and corporate strategies means that yesterday's decisions could be wrong today. While there are many factors at play in optimal management of a project portfolio, earned value management provides some quantitative data to help make the best possible decision. Using the analytical tools of earned value management to review and predict cost and schedule performance, managers can learn if a troubled project is turning around or just sinking deeper.

One of the watershed events in the history of earned value management occurred in the early 1990s when several large U.S. Department of Defense projects were cancelled relatively early in their schedule. Why? Because, among other indicators, earned value management data analysis said, "You can't get there from here." So, if resources are limited, time is of the essence, and customer expectations must be met, how does earned value management help project managers make the best decision?

Addressing the Cost Question

Earned value management lends insight into what work is being obtained for the money being spent. Both CPI and CV should be used when comparing projects side by side. A CPI of 0.9 is better than one of 0.8, but the CPI value reveals nothing about how many dollars are involved. Percent Cost Variances only indicate variance with respect to currently completed work. A cost variances of –$50,000 is smaller than one of –$200,000, but these variances hold little significance without knowledge of the project budget (BAC) and any contingency or MR. In addition, it is important to know if the project is near completion; if it is, then the cost variance might not change significantly. The Percent Complete indicates how far along the project is, providing insight as to the real impact of a decision to continue or cancel the project, or assign resources toward or away from the project.

Lastly, computing the EAC provides valuable cost information for decision-making since it is computed from knowledge of the BAC and cost performance to date. The table below shows how the cost data can be presented to provide a summary of EVM analysis products, and the question each column addresses.

EVM Term	Question	Project A	Project B	Project C	Project D
BAC	What is the size of the project?	5.00	8.00	15.00	25.00
EV	What is the value of the work done to date?	4.00	5.80	12.40	22.00
AC	How much has been spent doing this work?	3.00	7.00	13.00	23.00
CPI	How efficiently is money being spent?	1.3	0.83	0.95	0.96
PC	How much of the project is complete?	80%	73%	83%	88%
EAC	How much will likely be spent?	3.8	9.7	16	26
VAR	How far off budget is this?	1.3	–1.7	–0.7	–1.1
VAR%	How significant is this?	25%	–21%	–4.8%	–4.5%

VAR is the difference between the budget (BAC) and the current estimate of the final cost (EAC). VAR% is the difference expressed as a percentage.

Note that the accuracy of the forecast is limited to two significant digits and rounded up to avoid the suggestion of any higher accuracy in the analysis.

With earned value management in place, one common management error can be avoided—decisions are not based on how much has been spent compared to how much was planned to be spent. Instead, decisions use the concepts of Earned Value, Actual Cost, and Planned Value.

Addressing the Schedule Question

Earned value management also yields insight as to what is being realized for the days, weeks, and months spent on the project. To do this effectively, SPI_t must be used, as it accurately reports the schedule condition. As with CPI, an SPI_t of 0.8 is better than one of 0.75, but this does not say anything about how many days or weeks of schedule the SPI_t represents. Likewise, an SV_t of −3 weeks is certainly smaller than one of −10 weeks, but the significance of these variances is not apparent without knowing the project duration. In addition, just as in the preceding cost question discussion, knowledge of whether the project is near completion is critical; if it is, then the schedule variance might not change significantly. SPI_t and SV_t must be used for schedule analysis because conventional SPI_s and SV_s do not reveal schedule status as the project moves nearer to completion.

Calculating the Estimate Duration provides valuable schedule information for decision-making. It is computed using the earned schedule data so that it has relevance to the end of the project. Using the Planned Duration and the SPI_t, we can compute the expected duration of the project. The table below shows how the schedule data can be presented to provide a summary of EVM analysis products, and the question each column addresses.

EVM Term	Question	Project A	Project B	Project C	Project D
PD	How long is the project time line?	18.00	14.00	22.00	9.00
ES	When was the work now done supposed to be complete?	6.50	10.30	13.50	4.50
AT	How long have we been working on this project?	8.00	9.00	16.00	5.00
SPI_t	How efficiently is our calendar time being spent?	0.8	1.14	0.84	0.90
ED	How much time will likely be needed to complete the project?	22	12	26	10
VAR	How far off the time line is this?	−4.2	1.8	−4.1	−1.0
VAR%	How significant is this?	−23%	13%	−19%	−11%

VAR is the difference between the planned duration (PD) and the currently estimated duration (ED). *VAR%* is the difference expressed as a percentage.

Note that the accuracy of the forecast is limited to two significant digits and rounded up to avoid the suggestion of any higher accuracy in the analysis.

Using Trends in Decision-Making

Many organizations use earned value management data in tabular reports, listing Planned Value, Earned Value, Actual Cost, Earned Schedule, schedule variance, cost variance, SPI, and CPI. This practice conveniently puts all the data in one place and precisely shows data values. However, tabular data fail to show the vitality of the earned value management data. Using charts such as those illustrated in Figures 2-6 through 2-8 can give an organization a visual indication as to where a project has been and, more important, where it is headed. If the project is behind schedule, is the Earned Value line closing in on the Planned Value? Is it getting closer to being on schedule? If, at the same time, the Actual Cost line is moving well above the Earned Value, why is this occurring? Is overtime being used to get work back on schedule? Earned value management metrics do not often provide answers, but they show the questions that need to asked.

The Project Critical Path

Earned value management is a powerful tool. It should be part of every project manager's toolkit and every organization's skill set. However, using earned value management does not mean that other traditional project management tools should be abandoned. In particular, the critical path method of determining those activities that define a project's duration should continue. Typically, earned value management is applied to all project activities. It makes no distinction between critical path activities and others. Thus, the SPI can look good (close to 1.0) early in the project, even though a critical path activity is not doing well. This situation can occur because any work being done creates Earned Value, even if such work is not on the critical path. Sometimes project staff will start non-critical activities ahead of schedule just to get started. This practice can generate Earned Value that is close to the Planned Value. (It also can generate rework, since work started prematurely is not aware of product complexity learned later.) Project managers should always focus on critical path activities as well as review other project performance data to ensure the right work is getting done, and required quality is achieved. Even if the project manager ignores the critical path, the earned value management data will eventually reveal poor schedule performance. By focusing on the critical path, the project manager may become aware of potential schedule problems sooner.

It is also important to know that the work was completed to the required quality. The project network should illustrate the flow of internal products from activity to activity. One method to make sure the expected product quality is there, before declaring the activity complete and earning all its Planned Value, is to ask the leader of the downstream activity, "Can you use this product in its current state?" and "Do you have any concerns or risk associated with starting your task using this product?" Such questions can often illuminate quality issues as CAMs, often under pressure to complete work, may try to prematurely declare their work done.

Managing the Triple Constraint

Projects operate in an environment of a triple constraint: cost, schedule, and meeting requirements. The last parameter addresses project quality or the degree to which the customer need was met. Basic earned value management lets project managers know how they are doing on the first two elements. (Some advanced methods of computing Earned Value account for performance or scope. One such technique is Performance-Based Earned Value™.)[8]

Project managers need to know which *one* of the triple constraints is key to their stakeholders. (One of the three is usually critical; the other two are less so. For example, it is safe to assume that the 1999 Y2K projects had schedule as paramount, followed by performance. Cost was not a key constraint.) Earned value management data help in balancing the triple constraints by showing project status relative to cost and schedule and how to make tradeoffs. If the CPI is higher than the SPI, but schedule is more important, should more be spent to improve the SPI at the expense of a lower CPI? While earned value management cannot make decisions, it can indicate what the options are and, over time, show whether the desired effect is being achieved.

ACCURACY AND SIGNIFICANT DIGITS

Earned value management uses information from the organization's scheduling and accounting systems. Scheduling systems rarely have the detail and accuracy of accounting systems. Often, legal requirements dictate that accounting systems be accurate and auditable. Schedules cannot be as detailed as accounting systems or (1) the project would never get out of the planning stage and into execution and (2) project planners would convince themselves that they know a lot more about project work than they really do.

Moreover, most project work is difficult to measure. For example, a typical response to a work status question might be, "I think I am 30% done with the specification." Perhaps it is really 40%, or maybe it is just 20%. An answer of 35% suggests a slightly higher level of precision in understanding the whole task and what part is actually complete. An answer of 37% suggests an unrealistically precise measurement of an imprecise task—why not 36% or 38%? While some tasks produce a definitive total number of items allowing enumeration of the number produced to date, many project tasks do not allow such precision.

Project summary tables often list SPI and CPI with three significant digits, such as an SPI of 1.23 and a CPI of 0.977. Recall that

Earned Value comprises part of the calculation for both SPI and CPI. If the amount of work completed cannot be expressed in more than two significant digits, how can the SPI or CPI consist of three significant digits? SPI and CPI should never be shown with more than two significant digits. Round up or down to yield the nearest two-digit value (i.e., 1.23 would become 1.2 and 0.977 would become 0.98.) Otherwise, precision that is not there is implied.

INTEGRATION OF EARNED VALUE MANAGEMENT WITH PMBOK® PLANNING AND CONTROL PROCESS GROUPS

The Performance Management Baseline (PMB) is developed from the time-phased budget that, in turn, is derived from a resource-loaded and costed schedule. The development of the Performance Management Baseline is done within the PMI® PMBOK® Monitoring and Controlling Process Group. The Performance Management Baseline should be created at the close of the planning process. Periodic assessment of the project's Actual Cost and Earned Value is part of the PMI® PMBOK® Control Process Group and is included with Cost Management and Time Management.

Basic Concepts of Earned Value Management

- Percentage spent is not percentage done.

- Time spent does not mean work was done.

- Planned Value is the value of scheduled products, services, or activities paid directly by the project.

- Earned Value is the value of completed products, services, or activities based on Planned Value.

- Actual Cost is the cost of completing work.

- The cost of completing work does not change the work's value.

- Earned value management analysis methods include cost and schedule variances and percentage variances.

- SPI and CPI show how well time and money are being used, respectively.

- Earned schedule techniques create better schedule analysis than traditional schedule performance measures.

- Earned value management analysis can estimate cost at complete (EAC) and likely completion date.

- Cost and schedule variances are based on funds spent and planned work with respect to completed work, not the whole project.

- Trend charts show where the project is headed, while tabular data show precise values.

- Earned value management does not address product or project quality.

- SPI and CPI are only accurate to two significant digits.

NOTES

1. Walt Lipke, "Schedule Is Different," *The Measurable News* (March 2003): 10.
2. When capitalized, Earned Schedule refers to the unique parameters associated with earned schedule. When set in lower case, it refers to the earned schedule technique of earned value management.
3. Kym Henderson, "Earned Schedule: A Breakthrough Extension to Earned Value Theory? A Retrospective Analysis of Real Project Data," *The Measurable News* (Summer 2003): 13.
4. Stephen Vandevoorde and Mario Vanhoucke, "A Comparison of Different Project Duration Forecasting Methods Using Earned Value Metrics," *International Journal of Project Management*, 24 (2006), 289–302.
5. Maria Vanhoucke and Stephen Vandevoorde, "A Simulation and Evaluation of Earned Value Metrics to Forecast the Project Duration," June 2005, Ghent University working paper 05/317 (under submission).
6. David S. Christensen and Kirk I. Payne, "CPI Stability—Fact or Fiction?" *Journal of Parametrics* 10 (1992): 27–40.
7. David S. Christensen and Scott Heise, "Cost Performance Index Stability," *National Contract Management Journal* 25 (1993): 7–15.
8. Paul J. Solomon, "Performance Based Earned Value," Crosstalk, August 2005, www.stsc.hill.af.mil/crosstalk/2005/08/0508Solomon.html.

Requirements for Earned Value Management

When an organization's personnel say they do earned value management, it is important to know *how* they do it. If the firm is your subcontractor, you might rely on its earned value management performance reports to report how your project is going. If you are paying progress payments, you might use its earned value management data to set the payment amount. If the organization will be providing you a key subassembly, you might use earned value management data to increase staff levels in anticipation of its arrival.

This book discusses the Earned Value Management Maturity Model (EVM³).[1] Since a maturity model can be defined for earned value management (EVM), more or less robust applications of EVM must exist. Also, various national standards exist for earned value management, one being ANSI/EIA 748, "Earned Value Management Systems." This chapter discusses the absolute minimum requirements for earned value management to be of use and to provide meaningful project performance information. This chapter *does not* address all the requirements to meet various international earned value management system standards.

Certain enablers need to be in place for earned value management efforts to be effective. Without these enablers, the earned value management data will be of limited value; worse yet, efforts to implement earned value management will have been wasted. The four minimum requirements necessary to implement earned value management are:

- A sound schedule

- A time-phased budget

- A means of collecting progress information

- A means of collecting cost information

The first two you get from good project planning; the second two you get during project execution.

Of course, these requirements are not unique to earned value management. They are simply sound project management planning practices. If earned value management will be used to measure how well a project is being executed, doesn't it make sense to start with an executable plan?

GETTING TO A SOUND SCHEDULE

Earned value management is a means of measuring the ability to follow a time-phased budget and schedule. It has the unique ability to quickly show when a plan is bad or can't be followed. While cost and schedule variances are commonplace due to uncertainty and risk, nobody likes the attention caused by large cost and schedule variances. Thus, a basic tenet of earned value management is: Start with a good project plan. There is no substitute for a sound schedule and budget based on well-thought-out estimates of time and effort.

The project schedule should be developed through a sequence of activities similar to Figure 3-1. Once the statement of work is reviewed by the project manager, the skills and knowledge of the senior project team can be determined. Once these people are part of the planning team, they can create the WBS and

Figure 3-1. The Project Planning Process

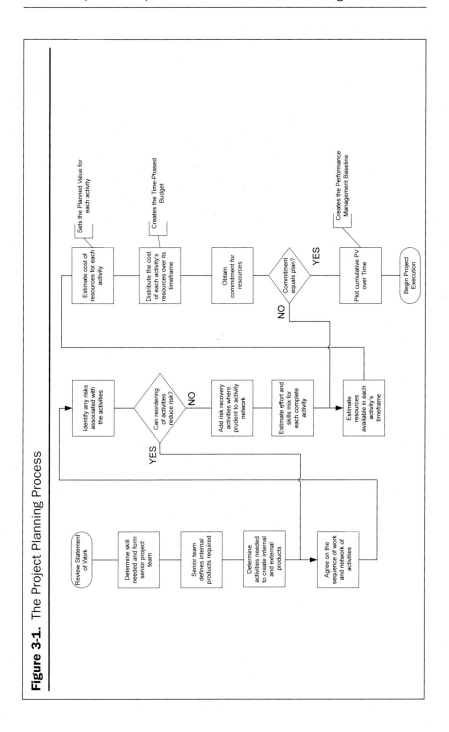

identify the internal products needed to develop the deliverable items. This step defines the project activities needed to produce internal and deliverable products.

While the general sequence of the required work products may be known, the exact network of activities to produce them needs to be developed. Risk management and other considerations should cause the evaluation of several networks before deciding on the network that balances the requirements of the project with the risks and complexity of the network. Dependencies and parallel efforts should be minimized where possible, while creating many small integration points versus a few large ones. Risk recovery activities should be part of the network so they are there if needed, such as when a test fails. In this way, if the test fails there is planned time to recover rather than just living with the resulting delay. If a test passes, the recovery activity is not needed and the schedule can be accelerated.

Once the best network is determined, the activities should be resource loaded with planned resources to determine the duration of the activities. Once these resources are committed to the project, the Planned Value and time phased budget for the activities is determined. The result should be a plan that is executable and tolerant of known risks.

The project manager might set some contingency funds aside. These funds are not included in the funds to execute the plan. If it becomes necessary to use contingency funds, doing so still will not cause expenditures beyond the total authorized project budget. In earned value management parlance, this contingency fund is called the management reserve (MR); it is not included in the Performance Management Baseline because it is not part of any planned activity. The budget at complete (which is the final cumulative Planned Value) plus the MR equals the project's authorized budget. This relationship can be expressed in a formula as

Project's Authorized Budget = BAC + MR   (Formula 15)

PLANNED VALUE: CREATING A TIME-PHASED BUDGET

A time-phased budget shows how much you expect to spend each period on the work scheduled to be done. Using the detailed schedule and resource commitments, it is relatively easy to get the time-phased budget. For each activity, you can estimate the cost of the resources for the timeframe in which they will be used. You do this for every activity over the project's timeline. Planned Value is found by costing out the resources at the time they are needed to produce a time-phased budget tied to the schedule (Figure 3-2). When plotted over time, the time-phased budget is the Performance Management Baseline introduced in Chapter 2 (see Figure 2-1).

This process also determines the Planned Value for each activity. It is simply the total value of the resources planned and budgeted to complete the activity. Adding the Planned Values for all the activities gives you the final value of the Performance Management Baseline, because the Performance Management Baseline is derived from the value of all the work within the schedule. Figure 3-2 shows a Control Account with five work packages. The BAC for the Control Account is 92. The Planned Value for each work package is the sum of its monthly Planned Values.

EARNED VALUE: COLLECTING PROGRESS INFORMATION

Periodically, usually monthly, managers must determine how the project is progressing relative to the plan. This assessment yields Earned Value. You cannot determine project schedule performance without a detailed examination of each activity in the schedule.

Figure 3-2. Control Account with Five Work Packages

Work Package	Mar	Apr	May	Jun	Jul	Aug	Sep	Oct
Work Package 1	2	5	4					
Work Package 2	2	4	7	7	3			
Work Package 3		1	4	6	4	6	3	
Work Package 4					9	4		
Work Package 5					3	8	8	2
Monthly Planned Value	4	10	15	13	19	18	11	2
Total Planned Value	4	14	29	42	61	79	90	92

BAC = 92

All activities fall into one of three categories:

- Not started

- Started and underway

- Completed

If an activity has not been started, its Earned Value is zero since nothing has been accomplished. If an activity is complete, then its Earned Value is equal to its Planned Value. If an activity is underway, then its Earned Value is approximated based on the amount of work done. This approximation is done without regard to the funds spent or time elapsed. For example, if 30 units out of 50 are complete, the activity is 60% done if each unit is equal. You could use this to compute an Earned Value of 60% of the Planned Value. If the work is less tangible, make the best assessment you can. There are several established ways to determine how Earned Value is estimated for partially completed work. These go by labels of "0%/100%," "50%/50%," "estimated percentage," "physical percentage," etc. Addressing each of these techniques is beyond the scope of this book. Appendix A provides a summary of common earned value management work-in-process measurement methods.

Earned Value is based on an assessment of work done. Making this assessment requires knowledge of the nature of the work, how it was planned, and what was accomplished. It is the author's opinion that Earned Value can only be determined through a one-on-one conversation between the person responsible for the work and the project planner or project manager. Several earned value management software products claim to be able to compute Earned Value based on the recording of costs (or staff-hours) against an activity. These products violate the basic ground rule of earned value management: Work completed cannot be determined by resources spent. It is possible that 20% of the planned costs have been charged to an activity, yet little or nothing is accomplished. Likewise, only 5% of the planned costs could be spent, but 15% of the work could be completed. As an alternative, some software products will conclude that an activity is 20% complete if it has been underway for 4 of the planned 20 weeks. With the exception of project support tasks that do not produce products, there is no reason to assume 20% of the work has been done simply because 20% of the planned time has elapsed.

Software vendors will suggest that if the activity leaders provide a current estimate of the time or funds needed to complete the work and the amount of time or funds spent, then a percentage complete can be computed. In the author's experience, when such estimates of additional time or funds are provided they are not based on any real analysis of the time or funds really needed to complete the work. As a parameter in calculating the real work done, these revised values provide little useful information.

An interview ensures that the Earned Value represents actual accomplishment. Say that, during the discussion, the activity leader is asked "What is your estimate of the percent complete?" The activity leader replies "Tell me how much I spent." The correct response to the activity leader, according to my favorite earned value management expert, is "No, you go first and then I'll tell you what you spent."

ACTUAL COST: COLLECTING COST INFORMATION

In addition to the Planned Value and Earned Value, you need Actual Cost to determine if what you spent resulted in an appropriate amount of work. In a relaxed earned value management implementation, staff-hours might be used as the unit of cost for labor-intensive tasks. If planning was also done in staff-hours, this can work. In any case, you must collect costs in a way that allows you to compare costs with the work done in the units of Earned Value.

On a small project or team effort, you might be satisfied with cost information for the whole project. This information would produce project-level cost and schedule variances, analysis products for the whole project, cost performance index (CPI) and schedule performance index (SPI), and a project's estimate at complete (EAC). However, data at this level will not allow you to use earned value management data to look within a project to determine challenged areas. While a hypothesis could be made as to why the overall project is in trouble, no earned value management data would exist to support it.

There is a very important point about the detail and precision of schedule information and cost information to consider. Most projects and organizations have elaborate and detailed project accounting structures to know *exactly* how much was spent on each task, commonly using a Work Breakdown Structure (WBS). This information, the Actual Cost, is compared to the Earned Value to determine cost variances and the CPI. Yet, the estimate of amount of work completed (Earned Value) is sadly imprecise, and usually relies on someone's estimate. The addition of more accounting numbers does not add more precision to the computation of CPIs; in fact, it might add to the error, as people often make mistakes when trying to guess the correct charge number from the many available. More charge numbers do not mean more accurate data; they might mean more detailed data, but they could reduce accuracy to a point where the hoped-for detail is lost.

To add precision to Earned Value without adding accounting complexity, most projects plan detailed work at one level lower than the accounting system. In earned value management terms, the detailed work is called *work packages*. This approach adds precision to the estimate of progress without adding accounting complexity. The sums of the work packages' Planned Value and Earned Value are compared to the Actual Cost at a higher level in the project (Figure 3-3).

Figure 3-3. Relationship of WBS Budgets and Work Packages

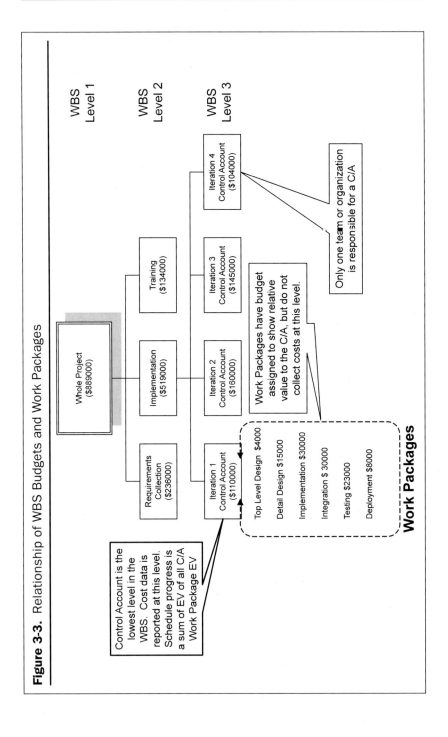

In deciding how much cost accounting detail is needed, you must consider two principles:

- **You cannot know the CPI to any more detail than you collect costs.** If the financial system uses dollars, dollars define the level of detail. Often, staff-hours provide more cost detail, but only in units of hours.

- **Planning should be done at a level lower than the cost-collection level by using work packages to add precision to the Earned Value.** This approach allows the Earned Value precision to be closer to the precision of the Actual Cost. (However, SPI can be computed at any level where planning is done and accomplishment can be measured, since Actual Cost is not in the calculation.)

Requirements for Earned Value Management

- A sound schedule is a necessary prerequisite to earned value management.

- The expected cost of an activity is its Planned Value.

- An activity's Planned Value for each month is determined during planning, not execution.

- A time-phased budget is simply the cumulative Planned Value of all project work, month by month.

- The Performance Management Baseline is a plot of the cumulative Planned Value over time.

- Contingency funds are not part of a project's planned costs; thus, they are not included within the Performance Management Baseline.

- The earned value management planned budget at complete (BAC) can be less than a project's authorized budget.

- Management reserve is the earned value management term for contingency funds.

- Earned Value is zero for activities that have not started.
- Earned Value equals Planned Value for activities that are complete.
- Earned Value is a percentage (or computed portion) of the Planned Value based on the progress of activities that are under way.
- Earned Value cannot be computed from hours or time spent on an activity.
- For labor-intensive projects, the earned value management cost element can be staff-hours.
- Earned Value is usually less accurate than Actual Cost; additional cost-accounting measures do not usually add accuracy to earned value management analysis products.
- CPI can only be computed at the level where cost information (staff-hours or dollars) is collected.
- SPI can be computed wherever values of Planned Value and Earned Value can be found.

NOTE

1. Earned Value Management Maturity Model and EVM[3] are registered trademarks of Management Technologies.

CHAPTER 4

Real and Imagined Impediments to Earned Value Management

Impediments stop many projects and organizations from implementing earned value management (EVM). This chapter discusses some of the most common obstacles—real or imagined—and suggests means to overcome the real impediments. Education, EVM pilot projects, EVM champions, and communication can go a long way toward reducing or eliminating common impediments.

The following table lists some common impediments. Each is discussed in this chapter.

Impediment	Real	Imagined
The ANSI 748 standards must be met		X
EVM is perceived as a personnel measurement scheme	X	X
EVM requires planning time and resources	X	
EVM is costly and time-consuming		X
EVM requires an auditable monetary cost-collection system		X
EVM requires a cultural change	X	
Executives must have an interest in EVM	X	
EVM requires a Work Breakdown Structure (WBS)		X

ANSI/EIA 748 STANDARDS MUST BE MET

A common imagined impediment is that all 32 ANSI/EIA guidelines must be met to perform earned value management. This is simply not true. While an ANSI-compliant earned value management system has significantly more utility, a simple earned value management system that meets only a few guidelines is quite useful as well. The original idea of EVM[3] was to express this idea through a maturity model that provided a graduated approach to meeting the earned value management standard. The hope is that more organizations and projects will adopt earned value management if they can do so simply, easily, and inexpensively.

Once an organization appreciates the utility of earned value management, it often initiates efforts to meet more guidelines in order to obtain even more valuable project insight. Part II of this book identifies the various levels of EVM[3] and the benefits of each

EVM IS A PERSONNEL MEASUREMENT SCHEME

This impediment can be real or imagined, depending on the management culture that exists within an organization. Earned value management measures how well a project follows its cost and schedule planning. Project planners and project managers might view this capability as a metric that management uses to measure their individual ability to plan a project and execute it flawlessly. For earned value management to be embraced as a project management tool, the organization must disassociate personnel performance measurement from earned value management project performance measurement. Project managers should be rewarded for the early detection of problems in the project plan, not for the ability to follow a flawed plan perfectly. For this to happen, an open environment must exist where the common goal of all concerned is to have earned value management data accurately reflect project status. Organizations that reward project managers based on project cost performance index (CPI) and schedule performance index (SPI) values of 1 or greater often find that raw earned value management data have been compromised. The end result is the realization that the project ends up overbudget or late when the EVM data gave no warning. The sad outcome is the abandonment of EVM, when the problem was the reward scheme, not the EVM system.

One common indicator of a reward system that is too EVM-based is the large use of level-of-effort (LOE) measures. LOE does not produce a schedule variance. (LOE is one of several common methods to estimate the Earned Value for activities that are underway. It should be used exclusively for project services that cannot have a schedule variance because no products are produced. Appendix A describes common methods to estimate the Earned Value for activities underway.) Another indicator is that milestones are completed on schedule, but the quality or performance in the related products is lacking.

EVM should not be used as the basis of a reward scheme. Instead, project managers should be rewarded for:

- Extracting utility from earned value management

- Minimal use of LOE

- Early recognition of planning or scoping errors

- Prediction of project end dates and final expenditures

EVM REQUIRES PROJECT PLANNING TIME AND RESOURCES

Earned value management excels at measuring how well the project team can follow the project plan. When earned value management shows large cost or schedule variances very early in the project, it usually indicates:

- The project planning was not completed.

- The project planning was flawed.

- The project cannot follow the plan.

These planning issues usually can be traced to a lack of planning resources and staff-hours, expertise, or time. Insufficient staff-hours, time, or expertise can result in a poor plan that does not reflect the project scope, consider the risks, estimate the time and resources accurately, or complete the planning before project execution begins. These problems are not unique to earned value management; they are common to many project environments. However, earned value management's ability to show quickly and quantitatively that a project is not following its plan suggests that good planning is even more important when deploying earned value management. Senior management has a role in the success of an EVM implementation in providing the project team the resources and time needed to develop a well-thought-out, doable plan. Functional management has a role in making good on commitments for planned resources.

EVM IS COSTLY AND TIME-CONSUMING

EVM is commonly misperceived as being costly and time-consuming. Once the investment is made in developing a sound, well-developed project plan, the application of earned value management is a small final step. The ANSI/EIA 748 guidelines do impose a large startup cost for integrating data that may not have been integrated previously. Nevertheless, obtaining the overall project Planned Value, Earned Value, and Actual Cost and obtaining the SPI and CPI requires simple and straight-forward computations. The estimate-at-complete (EAC) cost and completion date also are readily computed.

The author has implemented EVM using spreadsheets, a re-source loaded schedule, and a financial forecast in less than a day. EVM^3 identifies the minimal effort to perform EVM as EVM^3 Level 2. EVM^3 Level 3 and higher do require a significant investment. Using EVM simply to obtain a better idea of how a project is doing is not costly or time-consuming.

EVM REQUIRES AN AUDITABLE MONETARY COST-COLLECTION MECHANISM

To compute the CPI, cost data are necessary. Recall that the formula for CPI is Earned Value divided by Actual Cost. Whatever economic units are being used cancel each other out. Earned value management can still be used if resource consumption is considered a cost of completing project work. Labor-intensive projects like those for IT or engineering can use staff-hours to capture most, if not all, the project scope using earned value management. Using staff-hours has a distinct advantage over using monetary units for technical, labor-intensive work. Technical staff and team leaders often think in staff-hours. They use staff-hours to estimate work effort and can manage and control staff-hours. Often they review and approve weekly timesheets. If the technical staff were to address labor rates and overhead costs, they might feel less responsible for the monetary value.

Another advantage of using staff-hours as a unit of economic measure is that staff-hours consumed is immediately known when reported. If timesheets are completed weekly, and Earned Value is obtained weekly, earned value management analysis can be performed without waiting for financial reports from the payroll department. Some organizations perform weekly earned value management using only staff-hours so that they can immediately see any variances. They prefer to work with weekly staff-hours rather than wait for month-end reports only to learn that the first week of the month did not go well. Earned value management should be a proactive management tool. However, use of staff-hours alone will not meet the ANSI/EIA 748 standard and will not allow you to use earned value management to manage material and other pure cost items.

COST DATA MUST BE AUDITABLE AND ACCURATE

ANSI/EIA 748–compliant earned value management systems must have auditable cost data. In fact, having accurate cost data forms a part of several ANSI/EIA guidelines. Historically, corporations spend a lot of energy on integrating the earned value management system with the formal books of account in order to have timely, accurate, and auditable cost data. However, from a purely earned value management point of view, your cost data need only be as accurate as your ability to know the Earned Value. Earned Value is often determined from subjective estimates of work completed; some estimates are made for very intangible tasks. (For example, to answer, "What is your percentage complete in requirements definition?" accurately requires knowledge of how many requirements will ultimately be defined.) Cost Variance (i.e., Earned Value minus Actual Cost) is only as accurate as the estimate of the Earned Value, regardless of the precision of the cost data.

EVM REQUIRES A CULTURAL CHANGE

Using earned value management requires a cultural change. As stated earlier, earned value management might be viewed as a project manager performance appraisal parameter, and the consequences of actually using it that way are horrible. Earned value management also requires a shift in the way people think about time spent, money spent, and work completed. Just because time, money, or staff-hours were spent on a task does not mean work was accomplished. This concept involves a big leap of understanding, but making that leap is essential if earned value management data are to be of value.

Unfortunately, much of today's project management software makes assumptions about the completion of work based solely on hours or funds spent as a percentage of a budgeted amount, or based on some period of elapsed time as a percentage of the planned duration of a task. However, spending 30% of a budget does not guarantee that 30% of the work is complete—or 10% or 50%. There is simply no equation that can compute work done based on funds spent. The same holds true for time spent. Earned value management requires an independent assessment of what was accomplished, which should and can be made without knowledge of the funds or time spent.

EXECUTIVES MUST HAVE AN INTEREST IN EVM

As with any initiative, an organization's management must show an interest in EVM for its use to be sustained. Management personnel should understand earned value management terms and analysis products if they expect project managers and teams to use them. (One Fortune 100 CEO has earned value management analysis data as one quadrant on each of his one-page project dashboards.)

Earned value management can be one of the key metrics used in program management and portfolio management due to its ability to predict project completion dates and costs. These values should be reviewed against the original business case and continuous return on investment calculations to determine if the project should be accelerated, delayed, prioritized, or cancelled. EVM also can help forecast revenues, expenses, and profits for corporate financial statements.

EVM REQUIRES A WBS

The ANSI/EIA 748 earned value management standard requires the project scope to be decomposed. It strongly suggests WBS as the mechanism for doing so. WBS is also a well-adopted project management best practice; the author considers it essential for managing projects of any significance. It is also core to the PMI® PMBOK® Process Groups and Knowledge Areas. However, the term *WBS* does not appear in any earned value management analysis formula or graph. Earned value management is possible on a team-of-five effort that does not require any further decomposition. ANSI's requirement exists so that cost and schedule variances can be computed within the project as well as for the overall project. This capability allows identification of where project variances are the greatest. For a very small effort, a WBS is not needed.

Overcoming Impediments to EVM

- EVM can be done without meeting all 32 guidelines found in ANSI/EIA 748.

- People must know that EVM will not be used to measure them, or they will massage the data.

- Good project planning is a prerequisite to EVM.

- Simplified EVM does not require significant cost and time, but the prerequisite project planning may, depending on the current planning practices.

- EVM can be done in staff-hours for labor-intensive projects.

- For a non-ANSI-compliant system, cost data need only be as accurate as the estimate of Earned Value.

- EVM requires a cultural shift in how people think about how much work is completed and how that estimate is derived.

- Executives must show an interest in EVM data if they want personnel to generate the data.

- A WBS is not needed when only overall project performance is being measured using EVM.

▲

PART II

Implementing Earned Value Management via the Earned Value Management Maturity Model

Define ANSI-compliant vs. certified?

CHAPTER 5

The Need for an Earned Value Management Maturity Model

An earned value management system (EVMS) is a set of activities, methods, policies, and practices that is used to develop and maintain an earned value management baseline, measure project performance, produce performance variance reports, predict program outcomes, and, when justified, revise baselines. As an organization matures, the earned value management system process becomes better defined and more consistently implemented throughout an organization. The earned value management system also provides better instrumentation of the project and thus produces better data, resulting in more accurate analysis and better forecasts of project outcomes.

CREATING A SCALABLE MODEL

Rapid and widespread acceptance of earned value management as a best practice has led an increasing number of institutions, both in the private and public sectors, to express interest in using earned value management in their project management processes. Their initial research into the subject often brings them to the U.S. ANSI/EIA 748 standard for earned value management systems. This document contains 32 guidelines that must be met to have an ANSI/EIA 748–compliant earned value management system.

Too often, potential users see the 32 guidelines as formidable obstacles to implementing earned value management within their project or organization. While these guidelines are needed for a formal, robust, auditable earned value management system, implementation can be scaled down from these guidelines and still yield a system capable of providing useful information for project management decision-making and portfolio management.

It was with a scalable approach to implementing EVM in mind that the idea of a maturity model was born. The 32 guidelines serve to turn away many potential organizations and project managers who could benefit from earned value management. If, as an alternative, a project could make only a modest investment in implementing earned value management, the utility of EVM would become clear. In turn, this would spawn further investment in earned value management in order to obtain better decision-making data, and the organization would continue to move toward an ANSI-compliant earned value management system. The challenge in developing a model was to decide which of the 32 guidelines to attempt to meet initially and which to put off until later.

The five-step Earned Value Management Maturity Model (EVM^3) is a model for organizations to use in implementing and improving earned value management. Firms that already have an ANSI/EIA 748–compliant earned value management system can use EVM^3 to establish earned value process metrics and create earned value management system improvement plans. Those that are just beginning to use earned value management can use the EVM^3 to grow to an ANSI-compliant system; the EVM^3 is tied to ANSI/EIA 748 by establishing compliance with this standard as a necessary condition for achieving EVM^3 Level 3. Organizations that would like to try the concept of earned value management within teams or projects can determine the EVM requirements they need to implement the simplest of earned value management systems.

The U.S. Office of Management and Budget (OMB) recognizes varying degrees of earned value management implementation.

Its earned value management evaluation method in use through FY 2007 provided a score of 1 (no effective earned value management) to a score of 5 (ANSI/EIA 748–compliant implementation). Starting in FY 2008, OMB will evaluate earned value management effectiveness using an internal ranking methodology. Because OMB evaluates programs in nine other areas as well, programs may choose to attain a less-than-ANSI-compliant implementation while working to improve poor evaluations in some of the other nine areas. The EVM³ provides criteria for a partially compliant EVMS. (Appendix B presents the alignment of EVM³ levels with the previous OMB scoring criteria.)

MATURITY MODELS

How can an organization's capability to apply earned value management be measured? What subset of ANSI/EIA 748 requirements is sufficient to get an organization started in earned value management? How is it possible to know if a teammate or contractor has a competent earned value management system in place?

To answer these questions, the U.S. Department of Defense (DoD) published its earned value management standard (the Cost/Schedule Control Systems Guidelines, or C/SCSC) over 35 years ago. DoD next established a formal validation process to evaluate its contractors' earned value management systems using an onsite review and validation process. For subsequent contracts, DoD conducts EVMS surveillance to ensure that the validated earned value management system is being used.

In the 1970s and early 1980s, DoD found itself in a situation regarding its software development contractors similar to the one we find ourselves in today regarding EVM implementation. It had no way of knowing whether one software development company or organization was better than another at software development. Yet, some firms seemed, in general, to be more successful. With the rising cost and risk of failed DoD software projects, the Software Engineering Institute (SEI) was founded.

SEI undertook an effort to determine the processes used in firms with a better-than-average track record. From these efforts, a series of best practices was documented as a goal for software organizations to attain.

Both developers and customers sought to meet these best practices. Known as the SEI Software Capability Maturity Model (CMM®), this set of practices is known to improve an organization's ability to meet stakeholders' expectations in software development projects. The CMM® possesses five levels of maturity, with the fifth being the highest capability. CMM® allows customers and teammates to know the skills and practices of their software developers through both internal and external assessments of their software capability. Many organizations are moving from the CMM® to the newer SEI CMMI® (Capability Maturity Model Integration), showing that the fundamental concept of a maturity model as a means of organizational self-discovery, continuous improvement, and industry recognition of best practices remains valid.

Both software development and application of earned value management are process-intensive efforts. Therefore, the basic five-level CMM® model can apply to the development of a maturity model for earned value management—EVM³.

Chapters 6 to 11 describe the five-step EVM³. This maturity model, like other maturity models, provides:

- Users a step-by-step means to evolve an earned value management system

- Firms and industries a common framework for discussing the relative strengths of various earned value management system applications

CHAPTER 6

Overview of the EVM³

The Earned Value Management Maturity Model (EVM³) is a staged, five-level (versus continuous) maturity model. EVM³ Level 1 is the lowest level and EVM³ Level 5 is the highest.

Level 1: The organization has little or no EVM.

Level 2: The organization has a low-cost, yet effective, EVM system in place and can monitor total project cost and schedule performance.

Level 3: The organization's EVM is fully compliant with ANSI/EIA guidelines.

Level 4: The organization is strongly committed to EVM, with systems in place to measure and assess its earned value management system.

Level 5: Improving the organization's earned value management system is an ongoing project.

EVM³ LEVEL 1: INITIAL LEVEL

EVM³ Level 1 is the level of organizations with very limited earned value management or no implementation in place. This level provides a starting point for an initial implementation of earned value management.

EVM³ LEVEL 2: LOCALIZED/PARTIAL IMPLEMENTATION

EVM³ Level 2 is attained by an organization whose earned value management implementation is less than fully compliant with ANSI/EIA 748 but that might be sufficient for smaller projects or teams. Earned value management might only by applied to certain teams or functional areas within a project, or only at the total project level. Use of earned value management may be initiated by team leaders for their areas and not by the project manager. EVM³ Level 2 allows for a defined, but less than full, implementation that can provide valuable project insight with a minimum of administrative cost.

EVM³ Level 2 implementations generally meet some ANSI/EIA 748 expectations, including:

- Planning and scheduling the scope

- Maintaining a performance baseline

- Monitoring project performance and forecasting outcomes

The initial benefits of the EVM³ Level 2 earned value management implementation are worth the modest investment and establish a positive first use of earned value management. Positive results encourage further use of earned value management, additional investment in earned value management, and the goal of attaining higher levels of EVM³.

EVM³ LEVEL 3: ANSI/EIA 748–COMPLIANT IMPLEMENTATION

At Level 3 the EVM data gives the management team useful information about the total project and activities within the project WBS. Control account managers are expected to meet both schedule and cost objectives, and SPI and CPI values for each account help localize project challenges within the WBS. The ability to review the earned value management data and compute SPI and CPI within the OBS allows analysis of how the project organizational elements are performing their project work. The incorporation of indirect costs in the project cost analysis allows cost variances to be attributable to direct or indirect costs, thus making indirect cost centers accountable for their impact on project costs.

[handwritten: direct vs. indirect]

EVM³ LEVEL 4: MANAGED IMPLEMENTATION

[handwritten: quality & health]

EVM³ Level 4 adds requirements for measuring the *quality* of earned value management data and introduces metrics for measuring the *health* of the earned value management system. The goal is to increase awareness of areas where improvement in the earned value management system would provide more timely decision-making data, reduced earned value management system cost, and improved fidelity between the earned value management data and the actual performance of the project.

[handwritten: training pgm]

In addition, EVM³ Level 4 includes the requirement for an ongoing earned value management training program, an organizational repository for earned value management historical data, and the establishment of an Earned Value Process Group. These three additional requirements help maintain the earned value management system's maturity level and provide the basis for an organization to move to EVM³ Level 5.

EVM³ LEVEL 5: OPTIMIZING IMPLEMENTATION

The highest level of EVM³, Level 5 requires monitoring efforts to improve an earned value management system. It is project management of the earned value management system improvement project. This level uses the earned value management process data from Level 4 to establish and track efforts to implement earned value management system process changes.

[handwritten: monitor & improve]

Organizations with an ANSI-compliant earned value management implementation can aim to achieve Levels 4 and 5 to improve the utility, timeliness, accuracy, and cost effectiveness of their earned value management systems.

EVM KEY PROCESS AREAS AND THE FRAMEWORK OF THE EVM³

Each maturity level, except EVM³ Level 1, is composed of several Key Process Areas (KPAs). KPAs identify the processes that must be addressed to achieve a maturity level. The KPAs for each EVM³ level, except Level 1, include Organizational, Planning, Accounting, Analysis, and Revisions to the Earned Value Management Baseline. These are identical to the major categories of the guidelines found in ANSI/EIA 748. Higher levels of EVM³ maturity include additional process areas such as Training, Knowledge Retention, Process Measurement, Defect Prevention, and Improvement.

Each KPA identifies a set of goals considered important for enhancing process capability. Each industry and organization needs to determine how it will meet the KPAs. EVM³ and the ANSI/EIA standard do not impose any particular style of management. The KPA goals must be met, but how they are met is left to the organization. To attain a given EVM³ level, the organization should show continuing and consistent application of EVM processes across multiple projects that meet all the KPAs for that given EVM³ level. If this is achieved, the organization can be said to be performing at that level.

Organizations may be defined as a particular site, business unit, project portfolio, or other entity. The definition is set by the corporation or agency. Because the EVM³ requires written directives and oversight, the definition is usually consistent with established entities that normally establish other policies, procedures, or directives.

At higher EVM³ levels, a KPA may have more goals than it did at a lower EVM³ level. For example, a KPA may call for partial fulfillment of the ANSI/EIA 748 standards at EVM³ Level 2 and complete fulfillment at EVM³ Level 3.

Each KPA is organized into four sections:

Commitment to Perform: The organization demonstrates a commitment to implement the key process area through policy and/or identification of a key staff position.

Ability to Perform: The organization demonstrates an ability to implement the key process area through the assignment of sufficient resources and establishment of supporting systems and training.

Activities Performed: These are the activities an organization typically performs to implement the key process area. Fewer, different, or additional activities can be performed if the result still achieves the process area goals.

Verifying Implementation: Artifacts typically are found within an organization that has implemented the key process area. Fewer, different, or additional artifacts can demonstrate that process area goals have been achieved.

CHAPTER 7

EVM³ Level 1: Initial Level

A project or organization at EVM³ Level 1 is incapable of consistently producing earned value management data for its projects. Application of earned value management might be performed by a few teams or specific efforts within projects, but its management value is not generally recognized.

Level 1	• No or very limited earned value management • Occasional use at the team level • Frequent re-baselines and poor planning • Limited value

EVM³ Level 1 is the initial level; it is the level of organizations that do not use earned value management. Use of EVM, if any, is spotty and only through individual efforts. Because it lacks management support, earned value management may be abandoned in times of project crisis. Earned value management baselines are lost as frequent replans occur to attempt to show current project condition as the planned condition.

An EVM³ Level 1 organization has little or no earned value management in use. Any use is limited to individuals, small projects, or team efforts where an earned value management advocate uses its principles in attempts to calculate cost performance index and schedule performance index, even though precise planning and cost data are missing. The Performance Management Baseline may be the original time-phased spend plan without regard to the use of short-duration work packages. Earned Value is only subjectively estimated at the total team or project level. A formal means of accounting for funds or hours spent on the project might be missing. The user might be forced to estimate the hours used per reporting period for the Actual Cost. A WBS may not exist, and data are not easily rolled up; there is no capability to drill down to problem areas. The user appreciates the importance of earned value management but finds the organization neither appreciates nor encourages earned value management.

In an EVM Level 1 organization, earned value management is unrecognized for its utility, and there are no organizational procedures in place to define the process and expectations. Earned value management reports might be present, but they lack credibility, as schedule and cost data look good, but overruns and late deliveries still occur. Earned value management performance depends on individual capabilities and varies with the skills, knowledge, and motivation of the person performing it. Few, if any, earned value management system processes are evident.

THE EVM³ LEVEL 1 ORGANIZATION

Life at Blue Zephyr Technology Corporation was hectic. Projects were in trouble. Employees were constantly working unpaid overtime, nights, and weekends. Morale was low. Customers called daily to learn the status of projects and deliverables, and former customers had nothing good to say about Blue Zephyr.

Management decided that hiring a few more technical people with the right skills might help the company image and get projects completed earlier. Robert, who ran the engineering department and was responsible for all the projects in the company, started interviewing candidates. One applicant impressed him: Heather. She had been in the industry for five years and possessed the experience Robert wanted. In addition, her resume included project management training that the Blue Zephyr workforce did not have. As most company revenue derived from completing customer projects, Robert felt Heather's training might bring useful skills to the firm.

Heather accepted the job and soon found herself managing one of the six technical teams on a large project. Her project manager, Carol, reported to Robert. Carol, who just recently assumed this position, worked her way up the engineering ranks and possessed no project management training. Robert felt her success as an engineer identified her for a project management assignment. Carol and Heather got along well, although Heather felt her training in scheduling, cost estimating, earned value management, scope control, and risk management made her more qualified when it came to project management.

Heather quickly gained the team's respect. Heather appreciated their abilities, and they liked Heather's project management skills. Heather created something she called a Performance Management Baseline when the team completed its planning. At the end of each month, she asked the team to detail what has been accomplished. Heather didn't use financial data, because budget and cost data were not available at the team level. But she did sign off on her team's timesheets, so she knew how many hours her team worked each week. She used spreadsheets to create plots of her Performance Management Baseline and recorded other project data she called Earned Value and Actual Cost.

As the project proceeded, the scope of the project began to challenge the six teams. Apparently, Robert had underestimated scope when he sold the effort to his boss, Howard (Vice President of the Custom Solutions product line). Everyone recognized that the project was running late and assumed it would take more funds than planned to complete.

It was 11:30 A.M. Howard called Robert into his office. "How much is this project going to cost, and when is it going to be done?" Howard asked. Robert did not know, but promised to find out.

Robert called Carol to request a new cost estimate, giving her a deadline of the end of the next day. Carol quickly called a project staff meeting for 1 P.M., telling all six team leaders to bring their cost and schedule data.

At the meeting, Carol requested each team leader's estimate of final cost and date of completion by first thing the next day. Five team leaders complained, saying they needed at least a week to develop good cost and schedule estimates. Heather casually said, "My team will need a funding increase of about 17% to complete its work and the effort will run 9 weeks late." Carol was amazed, as were the other team leaders. "How do you know that and why are you so sure?" she asked. Heather responded, "I'm using earned value management. My cumulative cost performance index and my percentage complete let me be sure. The numbers work out to about 117% of my current budget. My earned schedule analysis says I need 9 more weeks than originally planned."

Carol adjourned the meeting so the team leaders could develop their estimates. As they left the room, Carol called after them, "Get me your estimates by tomorrow morning." It looked like a long day and night for the team leaders. Heather went home early to see her son in his first school play. Meanwhile, back at the office, the others discussed how Heather had outdone them all with something called "earned value management."

EVM³ Level 2: Localized/Partial Implementation

A project or organization at EVM³ Level 2 produces earned value management data at the total project level that reflect the project's overall cost and schedule health. The organization performs formal configuration control of the project baseline. Cost data might be in staff-hours or other units analogous to financial units. Control accounts might not be established within the project. Material and subcontract monitoring might not be done. Indirect costs are not likely to be separately budgeted or accumulated.

Level 2 :	• Earned value management data for whole project • CPI and SPI for total project • Direct costs are reported in staff-hours or dollars

Level 1 :	• No or very limited earned value management • Occasional use at the team level • Frequent re-baselines and poor planning • Limited value

An EVM³ Level 2 organization is interested in using earned value management. It meets some of the practices found in the ANSI/EIA 748 standard. Level 2 organizations meet the simplified criteria of

• Planning and scheduling the project scope with a Work Breakdown Structure (WBS)

- Budgeting costs to project activities

- Maintaining a performance baseline

- Monitoring project performance

- Forecasting project outcome

An EVM[3] Level 2 organization might not separately plan or record indirect costs, material costs, or subcontracted efforts in its earned value management systems. Thus, while a project can compute project cost variance, it might not be able to isolate cost variances to these project cost elements. In addition, an EVM[3] Level 2 implementation does not require full integration of the organization's financial system with its earned value management system or WBS. Actual costs need only be collected at the total project level and can be in project staff-hours or other non-financial units. During the planning phase, the Planned Value units (staff-hours, dollars) use the same units as the cost units so that variances can be computed. There are probably no control accounts within the project.

UNDERSTANDING EVM[3] LEVEL 2

EVM[3] Level 2 organizations realize the value of earned value management. While they might not have the resources to fully meet the ANSI/EIA 748 guidelines (EVM[3] Level 3), they recognize that earned value management is a useful tool for the project manager and senior management. They use a WBS to separate work into meaningful, manageable pieces. Their earned value management accounting systems might not have detailed project cost accounting, but they can establish an overall project Performance Management Baseline from project planning and an overall project Actual Cost (AC) from the accounting system. Planned Value and AC might be expressed in financial units, or staff-hours for labor-intensive projects. They might base Earned Value (EV) more on subjective measures than objective ones and might not use common earned value management measurement techniques. Determining EV likely relies on estimated percentage complete and some level-of-effort (LOE) techniques. EVM³ Level 2 organizations establish variance thresholds and do monthly reviews of variance. They calculate cost and schedule variances and analyze them at the project level. They keep their baseline up-to-date with formal changes to the project scope and funding or rescheduling activities.

EVM³ Level 2 organizations minimize implementation costs to the essential activities needed to achieve correct, if not detailed, project cost and schedule information. Formal earned value management training might not exist. One-on-one and on-the-job training and mentoring are the primary training methods. Spreadsheets might be used to capture the plan and performance data, perform earned value management calculations, and provide graphs. Control accounts might not be established. Since the EVM trained workforce is limited in number, the accounting system might not provide multiple project accounts, and the WBS does not facilitate control accounts.

At EVM³ Level 2, the application of earned value management is not widespread or uniform throughout the enterprise. Some projects or Program Management Offices (PMOs) use earned value management; others do not. There also is inconsistency in how earned value management is used. Yet earned value management works, even at EVM³ Level 2, because the project's schedule performance (EV) can be integrated with the cost data (AC). The lack of detailed financial cost data is not critical since EV is only roughly estimated at the total project level. It is the limiting factor in the accuracy of variance calculations, cost performance index (CPI), and schedule performance index (SPI).

For simple projects and small organizations, EVM³ Level 2 might be sufficient. It is certainly an improvement over project management without earned value management. EVM³ Level 2 provides some of the basic functionality of an earned value management system at little cost. It can be viewed as entry-level earned value management for firms with a goal of a full, ANSI-compliant system.

At EVM[3] Level 2, the organization can produce cost variance (CV), schedule variance (SV), SPI, CPI, and estimated final cost and completion date for the whole project. These project planning and control metrics can illustrate the value of earned value management to a reluctant workforce and skeptical management.

With its low cost and relaxed requirements, EVM[3] Level 2 can help overcome cultural resistance to earned value management. The benefits of earned value management will outweigh the modest cost, leading to a positive first use of the technique. EVM[3] Level 2 can educate the organization on the key principles of earned value management, the most important of which is: Work accomplished cannot be measured by funds or time spent.

EVM[3] Level 2 can help define the policies for a future, enterprise-wide, ANSI-compliant system description. And, EVM[3] Level 2 can help define the requirements for the selection of commercial earned value management software tools or the development of custom systems for deploying earned value management throughout the organization.

KEY PROCESS AREAS

The Key Process Areas (KPAs) for EVM[3] Level 2 are listed below. The KPAs that are a subset of the ANSI/EIA 748 standards are identified with the ANSI/EIA standard's paragraph number in parenthesis. (Some ANSI/EIA guidelines have been paraphrased to simplify the explanation. Appendix C provides the unabridged ANSI/EIA guidelines.)

Organizational Process Areas

▲ Goal 1: Work is defined, typically using a WBS. (2.1a)

▲ Goal 2: Who does the work is defined. (2.1b)

▲ Goal 3: The company's planning and scheduling are integrated. (partially meets 2.1c)

Commitment to Perform

Projects or tasks subject to earned value management are required by a directive to have a written charter, statement of work, or other written document defining the scope of the effort and deliverable products. For a large or complex project, the effort must be decomposed into smaller efforts that are assigned to the workforce in an unambiguous way using a WBS. The project WBS forms the context in which the planning and scheduling are done. A directive requires that the lowest-level WBS elements be associated with an individual responsible for the work.

Ability to Perform

Management provides sufficient time and resources during project planning for the development of a project charter or statement of work, decomposition of the work, and assignment of the work elements to the workforce.

Activities Performed

During project planning, the scope of work is decomposed and captured in a WBS that identifies all deliverables and all the supporting efforts required to create the deliverables, including efforts such as project management services, quality services, etc. The WBS might be designed prior to schedule development. The WBS also might be a product of schedule development, where summary-level schedules define the upper levels of the WBS. In either case, all the deliverables and efforts within the WBS are limited to those items directly paid for by the project. Thus, the WBS defines all the *direct* project work—no more and no less. Any project support or products provided by the organization and paid through pooled funds (possibly quality management, shared laboratories, shipping and receiving, etc.) are not typically included.[1] (The WBS should not be defined with a financial, cost-collection point of view. The WBS should be determined from a logical decomposition of the project work.)

At EVM[3] Level 2, budgets are assigned or derived for each WBS element. While Level 2 does not require cost collection per the WBS, the budgets are used to determine large efforts from small efforts. This sets the PV for each WBS element so that a given percent complete of a large effort contributes more EV than the same percentage complete of a small effort.

The responsibilities for completing the project work are documented in a defined, unambiguous way. Typically, using the WBS, each lowest-level WBS element is assigned to a person who is responsible for completing the scope of work assigned. A Responsibility Assignment Matrix (RAM) or similar method is used to associate the WBS work to specific responsible individuals. (This person does not necessarily do the work, but he or she is responsible for seeing that it is done, within the schedule allocated to this effort, and meeting quality expectations. If cost is collected at this level, this person is also responsible to complete the work to the approved budget for that work. The person might be a team leader, department manager, a subcontractor's assigned project manager, etc.)

Verifying Implementation

A WBS document exists that defines the decomposition of the project scope in a hierarchical way. There is sufficient level of detail to allocate scope, budget, time, and resources to a specific individual responsible for completing the work. (The level of detail might vary within the WBS depending on project needs.)

A document exists showing who is assigned responsibility for completing work identified at the lowest level of WBS detail. This individual might be a team leader or manager whose subordinates complete the project work.

The project schedule and project planning are integrated such that the project tasks, the WBS, and the budget are consistent with the work and performance periods shown in the schedule. The hierarchy of the schedule is consistent with the WBS. If costs are collected below the total project level, they can be collected per the WBS.

Planning Process Area

▲ Goal 1: The authorized work is scheduled, and the sequence of work and the significant task interdependencies are shown. (2.2a)

▲ Goal 2: Physical products, milestones, technical performance goals, or other indicators are used to measure progress. (2.2b)

▲ Goal 3: A time-phased budget is established and maintained. (partially meeting 2.2c)

▲ Goal 4: Budgets (funds, staff-hours, or other measurable units) are established for project tasks and subtasks. (partially meeting paragraph 2.2e)

▲ Goal 5: LOE activity is identified, and its use is minimized to efforts that are immeasurable or where measurement is impractical. (2.2g)

▲ Goal 6: Project financial reserves and undistributed budget should be identified and continuously monitored. (2.2i)

▲ Goal 7: The project budget is reconciled with the sum of all internal project budgets and management reserves. (2.2j)

Commitment to Perform

Projects are required by policy to create an activity network showing significant interdependencies and perform sufficient scheduling to determine the sequence in which project work will be performed. A schedule, derived from the allocation of resources to activities, is required. A time-phased budget is made from the anticipated costs of these resources and when they are expected to be used. The schedule identifies the physical products (internal and external) to be developed, milestones, technical performance goals (where applicable), and/or other means to measure progress.

Policy requires that all work be associated with products or milestones, where possible. LOE work is minimized. Project management must know the percentage (by budget) of LOE within the project.

The amount of financial (management) reserve and undistributed budget, if any, is documented at the start of the project and continuously monitored during execution. (Undistributed budget represents funds that will be allocated to specific WBS elements at a future time for in-scope work; it is not a reserve or contingency fund.)

Policy requires that project funds that are not allocated to specific work elements be controlled by the project manager or other identified project staff. Project management reserve(s) and/or undistributed budget are identified, and their subsequent allocation to work elements is controlled, documented, and tracked. The project budget must equal the sum of all allocated budgets, management reserve(s), and undistributed budgets. (Project budget may not be equal to contract value, annual budget amount, etc. Project budget is the planned not-to-exceed value and excludes profit or reserve funds held outside the project.)

Ability to Perform

If cost will be collected within the project, then management provides sufficient time and resources during project planning for an orderly distribution of project funds using the WBS. Time and resources are available for the detail planning of near-term work, and the development of time-phased budgets according to the work plan. Forms and processes are defined for the establishment and maintenance of the baseline budget. Management reviews requested baseline changes in a timely fashion and approves changes, when appropriate.

The organization provides sufficient resources during the planning phase to develop an integrated plan that results in a schedule showing the sequence of work and significant task interdependencies. The organization might provide an activity network template from which a project-specific network can be derived. The template shows specific activities or milestones required by management but not the project scope, such as stage or gate reviews, mandatory phases, etc. The project manager receives current or forecast resource costs so that networked activities can be assigned resources using anticipated costs.

The organization provides financial support staff to the project staff to ensure that the project budget and any management reserve are properly accounted for and can be reconciled.

Activities Performed

During project planning, the persons assigned responsibility for the lowest elements of the WBS may further decompose the work for their preferred management style. (For example, if a WBS element duration is six months or more, then some number of smaller activities and milestones might be appropriate. This decision and the duration threshold are left to the discretion of organizational policies and the manager's preferences.)

For each WBS element, the manager time-phases the anticipated expenditure of budget (funds or staff-hours) over the planned duration of work by considering what resources are required when and their planned cost. Doing so results in a time-phased budget for each reporting period that approximates the budget expected to be consumed in completing work for this time period. Therefore, it also defines the Planned Value for work completed during this time. When all the WBS planning is rolled up to the project level, it yields a time-phased budget for all project work. This top-level time-phased budget is the project Performance Management Baseline.

Management approves the time-phased budget, thereby creating a baseline. If necessary, modifications to the baseline (due to changes in scope, cost basis, overhead rates, etc.) are made using organizational forms and processes. This ensures a controlled, managed baseline throughout the project.

The manager reviews all planning for any LOE activities to ensure that they, in fact, produce no products and do not have measurable means to evaluate progress. The manager compares the total value of the LOE activity budgets to the total of all the scheduled activities to determine the percentage of LOE (by budget) for the project.

The manager adds the budgets allocated to WBS elements and confirms they equal the budget assigned to the next-highest WBS element. In other words, all the funds are accounted for in the planning found throughout the WBS. The sum of all budgets in subordinate WBS equals the total for the WBS (Figure 3-3).

Verifying Implementation
An approved activity network and schedule, and a time-phased budget, must be documented and approved for a project. For

each WBS element, the time-phased budget equals the budget allocated to the WBS element. Milestones, products, and other indicators of progress are identified. The percentage of LOE (by dollar or staff-hour) activities is known. Documents show the amount of funds, if any, held as management reserve (contingency) or as undistributed budget. Documents also identify who controls these funds. The project schedule is consistent with the funding. The planning effort yields a schedule that is useful for managing the project and is consistent with the funding available for the project.

Accounting Process Area

▲ Goal 1: Costs are recorded in a manner consistent with budgeting. (partially meeting 2.3a)

Commitment to Perform
Policy requires projects accumulate cost information consistent with the units (staff-hours, funds, etc.) used in planning. Policy states the minimum acceptable frequency for recording costs, which is at least monthly.

Ability to Perform
Management provides a sufficiently robust financial management system to allow recording of the resource usage or costs incurred for the overall project. The units of accounting are identical to the units used in planning (staff-hours, funds, etc.). The *total* project expenditures must be reported with an accurate, timely accounting system.

Activities Performed
On a monthly basis, the costs associated with project activities are collected and recorded. These costs include all the budgeted elements identified during planning. For example, staff-hours or the cost of staff-hours might be collected, depending on

which unit was used in planning. If labor costs were used in planning, any rates and factors applied to basic labor rates also are recorded.

Verifying Implementation

A system is in place for recording project costs, including labor hours and/or labor costs. Necessary calculations are made to accurately convert resource utilization data to the units used in planning (i.e., labor hours to labor cost, etc.). Costs within the project may be estimated, but the total project cost is known accurately.

Analysis Process Area

▲ Goal 1: Cost and schedule variance are calculated at least monthly. (partially meeting 2.4a)

▲ Goal 2: Reasons for significant differences between planned and actual schedule performance (Schedule Variance) and between planned and actual cost performance (Cost Variance) are provided at least monthly and in sufficient detail for program management. (2.4b)

▲ Goal 3: Managerial actions are implemented based on earned value information. (2.4e)

▲ Goal 4: Revised cost-at-complete estimates are developed based on performance to date, commitment values for material, and estimates of future conditions. Cost-at-complete estimates are compared with the Performance Measurement Baseline, and important variances at completion are identified to company management and included in any applicable customer reporting requirements. (2.4f)

Commitment to Perform

Policy requires that both Cost Variance and Schedule Variance are calculated and available to the project manager at the close of each month or more frequently. Senior management defines a significance threshold—that is, the amount of variance (as a percentage, in funds, in staff-hours, etc.) below which no root cause analysis is required. These thresholds differentiate significant variances from insignificant ones. Thresholds might vary from project to project and over a project's duration. Project managers must provide root cause analysis for variances that exceed significance thresholds and take action based on the variances and other earned value management information. Organizational policy requires project managers to estimate the cost to complete the project based on earned value management data and other factors known to the project manager. The project manager must explain any significant variance between the estimated cost to complete and the project budget at complete.

Ability to Perform

Management provides sufficient time and resources during project execution for the timely calculation of variances and the timely analysis of conditions causing these variances. Analysis of Cost and Schedule Variance is completed before the end of the subsequent month or reporting period (i.e., analysis of period x data is complete before period $x + 1$ ends). The project manager receives any information regarding resource costs or other factors beyond his or her control that might affect costs so that these factors can be factored into the manager's estimated cost of completion.

Activities Performed

The organization computes Cost and Schedule Variance shortly after the end of the month or reporting period. Computations are made for current period and cumulative variances. When variances exceed management-defined thresholds, the project manager performs root cause analysis to identify the underlying source of the variance. (If the variance continues beyond one reporting period and is due to a continuing root cause, a new analysis is not required.) Where possible, the organization defines what management actions should be taken to address these variances. If the necessary action exceeds the project manager's authority, senior management takes the action. Project staff, project managers, and senior managers understand the nature of root cause analysis. Management rejects analysis of variance that only reports symptoms of the underlying root causes.

The project manager computes an estimated project cost at complete (EAC) using earned value management data (primarily CPI) and other available information. The project manager compares EAC to the budget at complete (BAC). If the variance between EAC and BAC is significant, management receives an explanation of the cause of the variance.

The project manager, using earned schedule data, computes SPI_t, and the Estimated Duration of the project. If the variance between PD and ED is significant, an explanation is provided to management.

Management bases its actions on earned value management information.

Verifying Implementation
An approved document shows the variance thresholds to be applied to the project. Project management receives variance reports that identify the type of variance, amount of variance, whether the variance is current period or cumulative, and whether variance thresholds are exceeded (i.e., whether a variance is non-trivial).

Management-directed actions that affect a project, whenever they are attributed to earned value management data and analysis, are documented.

The project manager reports to senior management and others the current project EAC, PD, and estimated completion date (ECD). The project manager explains any significant variance from the project BAC.

Revisions Process Area

▲ Goal 1: The performance baseline is maintained and changed consistent with authorized changes to the project scope, budget, or schedule. (2.5a)

▲ Goal 2: A traceable history of revisions to the baseline is retained. (2.5b)

▲ Goal 3: Retroactive changes to work performed records that would change previously reported actual costs, earned value, or budgets are controlled. Adjustments should be limited to corrections of errors, routine accounting adjustments, directed changes from the customer or management, and changes to improve the baseline integrity and accuracy of performance measurement data. (2.5c)

▲ Goal 4: Changes to the baseline require appropriate approval. (2.5d)

▲ Goal 5: Changes to the baseline are documented. (2.5e)

Commitment to Perform
Organizational policy requires formal change control of the Performance Management Baseline whenever the project scope, overall budget, or final scheduled completion date are officially

changed. Formal control of Performance Management Baseline is also required if any changes are made to the detailed project plans for the project, such as internal budgets, completion dates, or the WBS. This policy requires maintenance of a change history, appropriate levels of approval for changes, and documentation of where changes were made within the project.

A policy establishes under what circumstances retroactive changes can be made to previously reported EV or AC and who is authorized to approve such changes.

Ability to Perform

Management provides sufficient time and resources during project execution for timely maintenance of the performance baseline. Management defines levels of approval for baseline changes based on the significance of the baseline change, promptly reviews requested changes, and provides timely approval decisions. Performance Management Baseline record-keeping tools exist. These tools provide a way to record why each change occurred, who approved the change, what WBS element was affected or replanned, how the WBS was replanned, and when (the date) the change happened. Previous Performance Management Baseline versions might be recalled for historical purposes.

Activities Performed

The project manager approves a formal document that defines the project's earned value management performance baseline. This baseline is used for measuring cost and schedule performance as the project is executed.

Policy requires that a defined process be followed whenever the performance baseline is changed. This process includes recording the reason for changing the baseline, which WBS elements were affected, the amount of the change (funds or staff-hours), and any increase or decrease in the total performance baseline funding due to the distribution of management reserve (the contingency fund) or undistributed budget. Some changes might simply alter the Planned Value time-phase for future work packages. The appropriate level of management approves changes to baseline, and these changes are quickly adjudicated.

Verifying Implementation

Documents define the current performance baseline for the project. The Performance Management Baseline incorporates changes in project scope, budget, or schedule since the start of the project. These adjustments are traceable from the initial project baseline to the current baseline. Changes in internal budgets or planning within the project are also traceable. The appropriate authority approves each change to the baseline.

THE EVM³ LEVEL 2 ORGANIZATION

Staff changes at Blue Zephyr helped expand business and grow the firm's reputation. Shortly thereafter, the firm won a major $150 million project from a new client. The project appeared to possess great follow-on potential. Howard, the Blue Zephyr Vice President for Customer Solutions, considered this project to be strategically important to the company's future. He instructed Robert to staff the project carefully.

Robert announced plans to interview personnel for this highly visible project. Carol knew this project was her next career step. She had been with the company for over ten years, was an experienced engineer, and had run some smaller projects. When Robert named Heather project manager, it caught Carol and everyone by surprise. In making the announcement Robert said, "Heather has demonstrated the skills necessary to manage this project. She has shown that she continuously knows the status of her projects' cost and schedule, and can accurately forecast its outcome."

Heather assembled the team leaders for the new project. They expressed a readiness to start executing the project, but Heather responded by saying they first needed to devise a sound project plan. She advised that this project was too important not to talk through the overall effort and develop a workable plan. Over the next few weeks, the team leaders developed a project activity network, schedule, and cost estimates for each activity. They walked through the project plan again and again looking for a better plan and lower risk. Then they were ready to work.

Nevertheless, Heather added one final planning step. She told her team, "I want to put the project plan into an earned value management performance baseline so we can track our schedule and cost performance." She explained how she would use Earned Value to track progress against Planned Value, and compare Earned Value to Actual Cost. Heather decided to apply earned value management to just the whole project to keep implementation simple and not involve the team leaders. There would be no control account managers and no control accounts. Heather felt she might fail if she were too ambitious in trying to apply earned value management at the team level. She knew that Blue Zephyr did not provide earned value management training; more important, team leaders needed to focus on project tasks, not a new system. Heather wanted this project to provide an earned value management success story.

As the project got under way, the usual variances from the project schedule and financial plan occurred. Heather reminded her team leaders that they had done a good job of planning, but that projects possess uncertainty that can cause estimates to fluctuate. Three months into the project, Heather and Robert had to present a project status report at Howard's quarterly project review. They both knew Howard possessed a keen interest in this project and they both were ready.

Heather allowed Robert to present the status. He displayed the Gantt chart, the milestone dates, and the project financials. Some activities were ahead; some were behind. Robert conveyed that the schedule looked pretty good overall. He expressed pleasure that the project had only expended $12 million thus far, even though planning had called for $14 million in expenditures by now. Robert finished by stating Heather was doing a good job.

Howard turned to Heather to congratulate her. Heather replied, "Thank you, Howard, but unfortunately the project is not in good shape. While we have spent $12 million, the value of the work completed is only $9 million. In other words, we are financially overrun. Moreover, the tasks that are behind schedule are more significant than the ones that are ahead of schedule. We need to take immediate action to correct project performance." Howard, surprised by her remarks, turned to Robert, saying, "Robert, if I had listened to you, I would have thought our project was in good shape. You need to get a better handle on this effort. By the way, do you really know how your other projects are doing?"

Robert was still smarting from these comments when he asked Heather, "How did you know that much quantitative data about your project?" She replied, "I'm using something called earned value management."

NOTES

1. The Project Management Institute bookstore (www.pmi.org) sells the *Practice Standard for Work Breakdown Structures*.

▲
CHAPTER 9
EVM³ Level 3: ANSI/EIA 748–Compliant Implementation

A project or organization at EVM³ Level 3 embraces earned value management as a key element of project planning, execution, and control. The project or organization establishes control accounts. The organization includes material, direct, indirect, and subcontractor costs in planning and monitors them during execution. The organization integrates the financial and scheduling systems with both the Work Breakdown Structure (WBS) and the project Organizational Breakdown Structure (OBS). Earned value management analysis can occur anywhere within the WBS and OBS. Project variances can be attributed to specific control accounts. The organization budgets indirect costs and reports them separately so cost variances can be attributed correctly to direct or indirect cost variances. The organization identifies managers of indirect cost centers and expects them to explain significant indirect cost variances.

Level 3	<ul><li>ANSI 748 criteria</li><li>Material, indirect costs, and subcontractor costs</li><li>Control accounts and control account managers</li><li>WBS and OBS integrated with cost and scheduling systems</li></ul>

Level 2	<ul><li>Earned value management data for whole project</li><li>CPI and SPI for total project</li><li>Direct costs are reported in staff-hours or dollars</li></ul>

Level 1	<ul><li>No or very limited earned value management</li><li>Occasional use at the team level</li><li>Frequent re-baselines and poor planning</li><li>Limited value</li></ul>

An EVM³ Level 3 organization meets the requirement of the ANSI/EIA 748 standard. (Some ANSI/EIA guidelines are paraphrased here to simplify the explanation. Appendix C provides the unabridged ANSI/EIA guidelines.)

UNDERSTANDING EVM³ LEVEL 3

Management has approved an earned value management System Description, or similar document, that defines the organization's earned value management process. Throughout the organization, there is a uniform application of EVM, subject to management-approved tailoring of the System Description to meet project-specific needs. (Organizations maintaining an EVM system that previously met the U.S. Department of Defense Cost/Schedule Control Systems Criteria (C/SCSC) should be performing at EVM³ Level 3.)

KEY PROCESS AREAS

The Key Process Areas (KPAs) for EVM³ Level 3 include the requirements of ANSI/EIA 748 that were not addressed in the EVM³ Level 2 organization. Moreover, those ANSI/EIA 748 requirements that were only partially addressed in EVM³ Level 2 must be fully met at Level 3. Attaining EVM³ Level 3 assumes that all the requirements of EVM³ Level 2 continue to be met. In addition, the EVM³ Level 2 requirements that were only met at the total project level now need to be met for each control account with a project.

Note: In the goals that follow, the portion not included at EVM³ Level 2 appears in italics.

Organizational Process Area

▲ Goal 1: The company's planning, scheduling, budgeting, *work authorization and cost accumulation* processes are integrated with each other using the project *work breakdown structure and the project organizational structure.* (2.1c)

▲ Goal 2: The company organization or function responsible for controlling overhead (indirect costs) is identified. (2.1d)

▲ Goal 3: The project work breakdown structure and the project organizational breakdown structure are integrated such that both cost and schedule performance can be measured for either or both structures. (2.1e)

Commitment to Perform

Organizational policy requires that a WBS decompose projects to a level sufficient for effective management. The planning, scheduling, budgeting, cost accounting, and work authorization are all integrated by means of the WBS and OBS (Organization Breakdown Structure) structures. Planning, scheduling, work authorization, and cost accounting are performed at the lowest level of the WBS within each WBS leg. (Not all WBS legs must extend to the same level.)

A project organizational structure (typically an OBS) identifies the project organizational structure and their relationships. The OBS and the WBS are sufficiently detailed that only one organizational entity is assigned each lowest-level WBS element.

The project manager must explicitly authorize the project work to be performed by the project's control account managers. Typically this includes the WBS elements identifier, with scope, start date, end date, and budget.

Written policy or a project document identifies the organization(s) or function(s) controlling overhead or indirect costs.

The organization's financial and scheduling processes allow project cost and schedule data to be accumulated and analyzed using both the OBS and WBS.

Ability to Perform

The organization invests in an integrated planning, scheduling, budgeting, work authorization, and cost accumulation system. The term *integrated* means that the data and information contained within the project activities are consistent throughout the WBS and OBS coding schemes. Integration does *not* require any degree of automation, shared databases, or software solutions. While it may be cost-effective to integrate the inputs and outputs of planning, scheduling, budgeting, work authorization, and financial systems through databases and an automated import/export method, doing so is not required.

The organization has a formal process in place by which the project manager delegates and authorizes work using the WBS and OBS.

This system is sufficiently robust to handle the most complicated projects that the organization might undertake, while flexible enough to be used by simpler, short-duration projects. The system identifies all project work with an associated WBS coding scheme. A group of personnel are skilled in administering and using the integrated system. They are available to support project staff efforts to develop and maintain the WBS, OBS, and cost and schedule baselines.

The project manager has work authorization templates that use OBS and WBS coding schemes such that OBS elements can be issued work authorizations using WBS elements.

The organization can accumulate earned value management data either by WBS or OBS, and at any level within these structures. (These multiple views of the project data are commonly implemented in a coding scheme that includes a project identifier field, an OBS field, and a WBS field so sorting and summation can be done either by OBS or WBS. See Figure 9-1.)

The project manager knows what organizational functions contribute to the project overhead (indirect costs) and who manages these functions.

Figure 9-1. Summarizing Data through the OBS and WBS

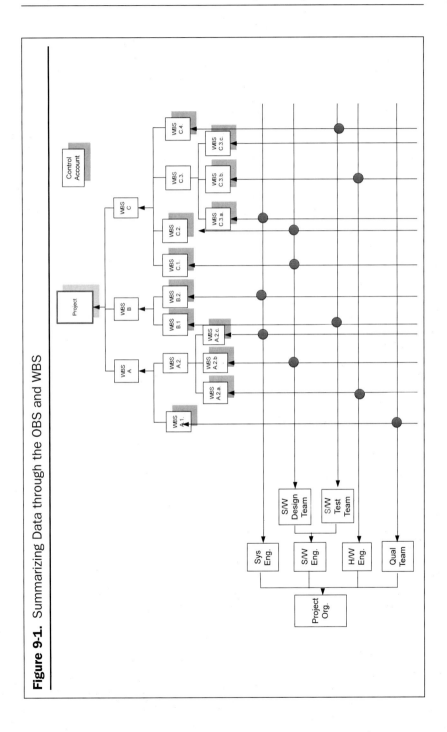

Activities Performed

During project planning, the project management staff and the functional management staff define a hierarchical decomposition of both functional staff and project work. This process yields both a project OBS and a project WBS. The functional organizational structure could remain unchanged for each project or could be unique when project teams are formed (i.e., integrated project or product teams and the like). This is largely determined by the project structure (functional, project, or matrix). Each project has a WBS that, at least at its lower levels, is unique to the project or type of project. Higher levels of the WBS might be defined by common project life-cycle phases or cost-collection categories. The organization accumulates cost and schedule data using both the WBS and the OBS. Summary level data is examined at each tier of the OBS or WBS to establish variances by work element (WBS) or organizational element (OBS) (Figure 9-2).

The project manager authorizes project staff to execute assigned work by reference to the WBS and OBS. This does not need to occur on an individual basis; rather, team leaders and functional managers are authorized to deploy and manage their resources to complete their assigned work.

Overhead (indirect) project costs are controlled by a specific organization or functional area that is responsible for associated costs and overhead rates.

Verifying Implementation

A project-unique WBS exists that reflects the specific scope of the project. Examining the lowest level of the OBS and WBS finds each specific WBS element assigned uniquely to a single OBS element. (Some OBS elements might be assigned multiple WBS elements.)

A document identifies and authorizes specific individuals, acting as team leaders or managers, to execute their assigned portions of the WBS. The document might include "start no earlier

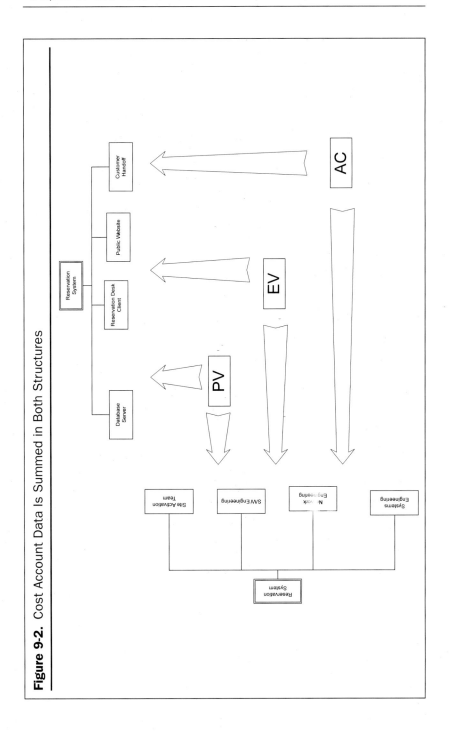

Figure 9-2. Cost Account Data Is Summed in Both Structures

than" or "finish no later than" dates and "spend no more than" information. Reference to a contract, statement of work, or other document might be present to add detail to the exact scope of work being authorized. The signatures of both the project manager and the person accepting the work (and budget and responsibility) should be present.

At least monthly, cost and schedule data are reported using, separately, both the OBS and WBS. The project-wide values of Earned Value, Actual Cost, and Planned Value are identical when summed via the OBS or WBS. (See Figure 9-1.)

The project manager can identify the person in the organization who controls overhead costs that will be incurred on the project.

Planning Process Area

▲ Goal 1: A time-phased budget is established and maintained *for each control account.* (2.2c)

▲ Goal 2: Significant cost elements (labor, material, etc.) are identified as needed for internal management and for control of subcontractors. (2.2d)

▲ Goal 3: Budgets (funds, staff-hours, or other measurable units) are established for control accounts and/or discrete work packages. Planning packages might be used for far-term efforts. (2.2e)

▲ Goal 4: Work package budgets sum to the control account budget. (2.2f)

▲ Goal 5: Overhead budgets are established for each significant organizational component for indirect expenses. Amounts in overhead pools to be allocated to the program as indirect costs are budgeted and identified. (2.2h)

Commitment to Perform

At EVM³ Level 3, the planning activities of EVM³ Level 2 extend to project control accounts. Organizational policy requires that control accounts be established within the project WBS, and control account managers must be assigned. The control account manager can reference his or her work authorization document to know what work is to be done, by when, for how much money (or staff-hours), and what is to be delivered. Each control account manager must plan project activities consistent with higher-level project dependencies, work authorizations, and requirements and produce a time-phased budget for his or her control account.

A financial planning policy requires that projects identify the cost elements necessary for effective internal management and control of subcontracts. These cost elements could be labor costs, material costs, overhead costs, subcontractor costs, and other costs that must be included in planning the total cost of the project.

Policy requires that budgets be established for indirect costs and that the cost allocation to the project be identified.

Organizational policy requires that control account managers receive or be assigned budgets for their control accounts or for the work packages within the control accounts. Planning packages are allowed under circumstances that are defined in a published policy. If work packages are used, then the budgets assigned to work packages sum to the budget for the control account. In other words, control account managers cannot hold any budget reserves at the control account level.

The organization identifies those organizational components that will become overhead expenses to the project and defines budgets for these overhead components. The organization defines the portion of the overhead budget that will be levied on projects so that project managers can accurately plan their budgets to include these overhead expenses. If overhead expenses are applied at the control account level, then control account managers have the overhead budget data to plan their costs accurately.

Ability to Perform

This is a continuation of the development of a time-phased budget from EVM³ Level 2. At EVM³ Level 3, the project time-phased budget is derived from lower-level planning done at the control account level. That is, summing all the time-phased budgets of control accounts results in the overall project time-phased budget. Each control account budget has a time-phased budget to measure its performance. The performance of all control accounts serves as the basis for overall project performance.

Control account managers have sufficient planning resources to produce an accurate time-phased budget for their control account(s). Resources should include time to develop comprehensive work plans using networked activities within their control account and networked dependencies to other control accounts, to ensure consistency with overall project milestones and deliverables. In addition, control account managers should possess forward-looking resource cost information so that they can accurately plan the expected cost of these resources at the planned point in time of usage. Control account managers have resources to capture and record the time-phased budget.

Project manager and control account managers know the organization's chart of accounts or cost elements. Thus, they can plan their control accounts using these cost elements and know that actual costs will be recorded using the same elements. This provision permits analysis of cost variances to the elements of cost.

Control account managers have time to decompose control accounts to work packages and allocate control account budgets to these work packages. They possess methods to identify planning packages different from work packages. Audits of control account manager planning show that the entire control account budget is distributed to work packages (if used). (Therefore, any control account containing any work packages must use all the control account budget in work packages.)

Managers of functions or organizations that contribute to overhead or indirect costs have resources to effectively plan their activities such that they can perform their functions within defined budgets.

Activities Performed

Control account managers develop detailed work package schedules that meet the overall objectives of the control account deliverables, timeline, and budget. The control account manager assigns a budget for each work package based on the estimated cost of resources needed to complete the work. The sum of the budgets assigned to the work packages exactly equals the control account budget. While cost information might only be collected at the control account level, assigning a budget to work packages within the control account allows them to be weighted in importance so that completion of a large work package contributes more Earned Value than completion of a small work package.

At the control account level, budgets for labor, materials, and other cost elements are developed. The cost elements are identical to the costs available from the financial system such that overall control account cost variances can be attributed to these elements of cost for effective management.

When a work package will not start for a long time, the control account manager can decide to hold it as a planning package. This action requires that the planning package be allocated its share of the control account budget and its timeframe be approximated. It is not detail planned (month by month) until it becomes a near-term work package, or more detail becomes known about the work.

The control account manager obtains forward-looking overhead rates and applies these rates to planning such that the control account budget includes these anticipated rates. If the financial system separately reports the various overhead costs, then the control account manager plans each of these costs such that cost variance can be attributed to the correct overhead account.

Verifying Implementation

Each project control account can produce a time-phased budget for the work within the control account. This budget is composed of cost elements that are available to the control account manager from the financial system. Subcontractor planned costs (payments) are identified at the time the subcontractor services or products will be used by the project. (*Note:* This time is likely earlier than when the project financial reports show the invoice as being paid.)

Where work packages are used, the control account time-phased budget equals the work package budgets plus any planning package budgets. In addition, the monthly control account time-phased budget equals the sum of all work package Planned Value for the month.

Planning packages are used when needed, and each has a budget assigned from the control account budget. A planning package can exist at the control account level if all the associated work is still distant.

Accounting Process Area

▲ Goal 1: A control account's direct costs are summarized to the WBS level without a single control account being allocated to more than one WBS element. (2.3b)

▲ Goal 2: A control account's direct costs are summarized to the contractor's organizational elements without a single control account being allocated to more than one OBS element. (2.3c)

▲ Goal 3: All contract-allocated (project-allocated) indirect costs are recorded. (2.3d)

▲ Goal 4: Unit costs, equivalent unit costs, or lot costs are identified when needed. (2.3e)

▲ Goal 5: Material accounting system subgoals are

   a. A control account's material accounting is summarized and assigned consistent with the budgets using recognized, acceptable, costing techniques.

   b. A control account's cost performance measurement is done at the most suitable point in time for each category of material, but not before progress payments or actual receipt of material.

   c. All material purchased for the program, including the residual inventory, is accounted for. (2.3f)

Commitment to Perform

The organization's financial accounting system provides direct cost information at the control account level. The costs associated with the control account are unique to only that control account (i.e., accounting is to the lowest level of the WBS, and each has a unique accounting number).

The organization's financial accounting system also provides direct cost information per the OBS. The costs associated with the WBS element(s) are unique to that OBS alone (i.e., no WBS element is associated with more than one OBS element).

The project receives financial reports showing indirect costs incurred by the project in the same cost elements as used in planning.

The financial reporting system provides per-unit costs, equivalent-unit costs, or per-lot costs when necessary for effective management of project material. For example, if the project will be charged for material from a common material pool, then the project can determine how much that material cost.

Financial policy and processes provide for material cost accounting using commonly accepted costing techniques. Cost of material is allocated to the project at the most appropriate time for the category of material (i.e., major purchase, lots, line stock, etc.) but not prior to progress payments to vendors or actual receipt of material.

Policy requires that all material purchased for the project be accounted for, including residual material, scrap, and waste.

Ability to Perform

Project managers have access to a financial accounting system that is sufficiently robust to accumulate and report costs using a WBS. (The access can be direct or through the help of financial analysts.) Costs can be recorded at the lowest level in the WBS and summarized to any higher-level WBS element. Financial reports at each WBS level separately identify individual elements of cost, such as labor-hours, labor rates, material cost, labor overhead, material overhead, and other project costs (other direct costs). For material items, the financial system can relate costs to per-unit, per-lot, or equivalent-unit costs.

The financial system also records cost and summarizes costs using the project's OBS. Where applicable, the reported elements of costs are identical to those reported in the WBS.

The project manager can access a material inventory system that provides accurate accounting of all project material purchased, used, scrapped, and wasted. The cost of material in each category is known.

Activities Performed

Monthly, or more often, control account managers obtain cost information related to their control account(s). This information includes direct costs reported in the same units used in planning. Managers of project organizational entities (teams, departments, etc.) also receive financial data reported in the same elements of costs. If material is used from pooled material or material lots, then the equivalent cost of material used is reported to the project and to those control accounts using the material.

The project manager receives reports of indirect project costs.

Control account managers associate the actual cost of material used with the point in time the Earned Value is recorded for the use of the material. The point of use can be when received or when used. When the actual cost of material is not known due to vendor invoicing delays, payment delays, or recording of cost to the project, the control account manager may estimate the actual cost for earned value management cost performance analysis. When the actual costs for the material become known, those values replace the estimated costs.

The project manager and others, as needed, receive reports showing all material purchased for the program, the amount of material used, and the amount remaining.

Verifying Implementation

Monthly, or more often, control account managers and project organizational managers receive reports that provide them direct cost information. The financial reports record costs in the same units and elements used in project planning. The costs reported only show the costs incurred for the work within the control account.

The costs for each lowest-level WBS can be found in only one control account and in only one OBS element. This is illustrated in Figure 9-2. Control accounts are at the WBS-OBS intersections, indicated by a black circle. Note that while an OBS element may have several control accounts, each control account has a unique WBS.

The project manager and control account manager, if necessary, receive a report showing indirect costs to the project. These reports categorize costs into the same indirect cost elements used when budgeting the indirect costs during planning. The control account manager receives a report on indirect costs if the control account manager pays for these costs at the control account level.

When material is used from pooled material or material lots, the cost of material used by the project is reported. These reports show the appropriate amount of material cost for the period by applying a unit cost or equivalent unit cost to the amount of material used. If an entire lot is used in one period, then the report reflects lot costs.

Control accounts show material actual costs at the point most appropriate for the material. Typically, this is at the time of consumption by the project. It cannot be earlier than material receipt or progress payments for the material. The intent is for material costs to be recorded as Actual Costs at the time the associated material's Earned Value is credited. This point in time differs from when actual payments are made to the vendor or shown in the accounting system. Therefore, control account managers often estimate the cost of material in the month they record the material Earned Value and then retroactively correct the value to the actual invoiced and paid amount when it is known.

The project manager and, if necessary, the control account manager receive reports showing material used and material remaining.

Analysis Process Area

▲ Goal 1: A *control account's* (and other required levels) cost and schedule variance are computed at least monthly *using actual cost data, or reconcilable cost data, from the accounting system.* (2.4a)

▲ Goal 2: Budgeted and applied (or actual) indirect costs are identified, and reasons for significant variances are provided at the level and frequency needed by management for effective control. (2.4c)

▲ Goal 3: Data elements and associated variances are summarized throughout the program organization and/or WBS as needed to support management and any required contractual customer reports. (2.4d)

Commitment to Perform

Organizational policy requires that each control account provide an analysis of cost and schedule variances using data from the accounting system or data that can be reconciled with the accounting data. This commitment expands on the commitment at EVM³ Level 2 by requiring control account managers to compute cost and schedule variances using earned value management data for the control account. Control account managers must perform root cause analysis of any variances that exceed management-defined thresholds. In addition, policy requires that overhead or indirect costs be collected and analyzed and variances from the planned overhead or indirect costs be understood.

Policy also requires that detailed project cost and schedule information be summarized at various levels of the OBS and WBS. Cost and schedule variances computed at these levels provide summary level variance for management visibility and/or customer insight.

Ability to Perform

Management provides resources and time to complete earned value management analysis tasks including calculation and analysis of cost and schedule variance on a monthly basis using data from the accounting system. Project managers have time to analyze significant cost and schedule variances for direct costs, and cost variance for indirect cost variances. Established means exist for the production of summary level reports by the WBS and OBS for internal and customer reports. Control account managers receive earned value management data for their control accounts and have the time to perform root cause analysis of significant variances.

Activities Performed

Control account managers compute control account variances monthly or more often based on actual cost data or data that can be reconciled with the general books of account. These data are used to compute cost and schedule variances as well. Control account managers perform analysis of significant variances and produce written reports for management that identify the root cause of variances and any corrective actions needed (if possible).

Variances in the planned versus actual indirect costs of the project are computed. Any significant variances are explained. The project manager or control account manager performs this indirect cost variance analysis, depending on where the indirect costs are recorded. The person or organization identified as having control over the indirect costs, as identified under "Planning Process Area" in EVM[3] Level 3, provides the reasons for the variance.

Earned Value, Actual Cost, and Planned Value are summarized using both the WBS and OBS. This summary yields identical values for these earned value management terms at the top level of both the WBS and the OBS. When significant variances occur at a given WBS or OBS level, additional analysis might occur above the control account level.

Verifying Implementation

Each control account manager is given or can produce cost variances using actual cost data or reconcilable cost data. Schedule variances are computed from the control account manager's assessment of the control account's Earned Value and Planned Value. Historical evidence shows that cost and schedule variances are computed at least monthly. The organization possesses variance analysis produced by the control account manager for all instances where cost or schedule variance exceeded management-defined thresholds.

The project manager receives indirect costs reports, as does the control account manager if necessary. The actual indirect costs are compared to the planned indirect costs. Variances are computed and root causes of significant indirect cost variances are provided to management.

As needed by management or customers, reports are organized by the WBS structure and the OBS structure that identify earned value management data and variances at the levels within the structure. Values at the top level of the WBS and OBS are identical.

Revisions Process Area

There are no additional goals for the revisions process area at EVM³ Level 3. However, EVM³ Level 3 generally adds significant complexity to an EVM³ Level 2 earned value management system. EVM³ Level 3 introduces control accounts; control account managers; work packages; detail elements of costs; and the planning of material costs, other direct costs, and indirect costs. Revisions in any of these elements need to be managed through the revision control process.

THE EVM³ LEVEL 3 ORGANIZATION

Blue Zephyr's business grew quickly as the number of satisfied customers grew. Now, Blue Zephyr's greatest challenge was managing all of its projects, particularly those that relied on common resources or products. A more consistent method of project management was needed, as was better information to manage Blue Zephyr's portfolio of projects.

Howard instituted a Program Management Office (PMO) to help manage the portfolio. He also created a new division focused on government customer solutions. That was when Blue Zephyr started to see requirements for earned value management in the Requests for Proposals. Blue Zephyr was finding that project management scoring was partially based on the use of an earned value management system. Overall scoring was tied to the ANSI/EIA 748 guideline. Howard knew that if Blue Zephyr was to succeed in acquiring government business, it needed an ANSI/EIA 748–compliant earned value management system.

Howard called Robert into his office, "You have been running our engineering department and overseeing our projects since the company was founded, but it's time we set up a PMO. I've decided that Heather will run the PMO. Her training and experience in project management are invaluable. Projects, not operations, are how we can make money in this business. From now on, you will be the engineering functional manager reporting to Heather, and she will be reporting to me." Robert left Howard's office wondering why the project management methods he had used for years no longer seemed adequate.

Heather quickly got to work in her new position. She held a staff meeting with all her project managers, including Carol. Those working in the new government business unit were familiar with the earned value management requirement, but everyone was surprised when Heather stated that all projects would begin using earned value management, adding that full compliance with ANSI/EIA 748 was the ultimate goal. "This is not just to win government business," Heather explained. "This approach will keep us informed on all our projects. Also, I want all team leaders using earned value management so they will be better prepared to become project managers. From now on, team leaders will be the control account managers on their projects."

Carol objected to this plan, saying, "I'm not on a government project. This earned value management takes too much time to set up, and I don't have the time to do the necessary project planning. I need to do the project work. I can't see the value in it." Heather explained that project planning is doing project work and that applying earned value management takes little time if planning is done well. Carol left the meeting unconvinced.

Time proved both of Howard's decisions—setting up a PMO and naming Heather to run it—correct. It also was clear that company-wide use of earned value management had paid off. Blue Zephyr achieved certification as being ANSI/EIA 748 compliant. More and more of the firm's government proposals landed new projects and more work.

At an all-hands meeting, Howard said, "Blue Zephyr could never have taken on so many projects and run them so well without Heather and her earned value management initiative. She directly helped the company attain its current level of government solutions contracts."

Earned value management analysis was used to set some of the color coding on Howard's stoplight charts to allow him to see where projects were headed. Also, he could monitor the company's control of overhead expenses better since they, too, were being tracked as a project cost using Blue Zephyr's ANSI/EIA 748–compliant earned value management system.

Howard liked the fact that control account managers were gaining experience in project planning, earned value management, and team skills. There were some promising future project managers within this group. His only frustration was that Carol's project never reported earned value management data. He knew Carol had already spent funds beyond her budget, but she reported it was close to being on schedule. When the customer called to complain about late deliveries on Carol's project, Howard knew action was needed. He called her and Robert into his office. Howard told Carol she was being assigned to Robert's engineering department, where she had started her career. "I've asked Heather to find a new project manager for your project," Howard said. "I don't need any more surprise calls from customers. I need to get earned value management data."

CHAPTER 10

EVM³ Level 4: Managed Implementation

The EVM³ Level 4 organization is interested in how well its earned value management system is operating. It collects earned value management system *performance* data and lessons learned in an earned value management repository. (Performance data measure how the earned value management system is performing, not how projects are performing.) The repository includes not only projects' earned value management data, but also metrics on the earned value management system itself. This activity is separate from reporting on project performance using earned value management.

Level 4
- Earned value management process group
- EVMS performance data
- Earned value management system training
- Earned value management library

Level 3
- ANSI 748 criteria
- Material, indirect costs, and subcontractor costs
- Control accounts and control account managers
- WBS and OBS integrated with cost and scheduling systems

Level 2
- Earned value management data for whole project
- CPI and SPI for total project
- Direct costs are reported in staff-hours or dollars

Level 1
- No or very limited earned value management
- Occasional use at the team level
- Frequent re-baselines and poor planning
- Limited value

UNDERSTANDING EVM³ LEVEL 4

The EVM³ Level 4 organization wants to improve its earned value management system processes. The organization possesses an organizational entity to define and improve the earned value management system process—an Earned Value Process Group (EVPG). A formal, ongoing employee-training program exists for instructing staff about earned value management system processes, tools, and implementation guidelines. An earned value management system library captures earned value management system lessons and reference material. The organization integrates changes to its project planning, project organization, scheduling, and funding processes with the earned value management system processes and makes the required changes in the earned value management system.

The EVM³ Level 4 organization possesses a robust ANSI/EIA 748 earned value management system and seeks to improve it. As with any process-improvement initiative, the first step is to obtain metrics on the process. As an EVM³ Level 4 organization, it already has moved from simply collecting earned value management data for project performance to collecting data on the earned value management system process itself. The organization retains metric data in a database for analysis and trending. These data measure such aspects of the earned value management system as the quality and timeliness of a project's earned value management data. This is used to help determine how the earned value management system is functioning and improving as a process.

KEY PROCESS AREAS

Training Process Area

▲ Goal 1: Training activities are planned.

▲ Goal 2: Training is provided for developing the skills and knowledge needed to perform earned value management.

Commitment to Perform

The organization develops and schedules earned value management training, including training in its company-specific EVM implementation, as described in earned value management description documents. The organization requires completion of specific earned value management training for project managers and team leaders before assigning them to projects using earned value management. The organization uses completion requirements to ensure students have acquired an effective level of understanding.

Ability to Perform

The organization provides resources to develop and maintain an earned value management system training program, including instructors, materials, and facilities. The training program has sufficient resources to meet the needs of projects in providing earned value management–trained control account managers, organizational managers, and project managers. Training may be periodic or just in time. The training protocol is kept current with changes made to the earned value management system processes.

Funding is provided for students to attend training and employees are given time to attend training.

The organization establishes earned value management knowledge standards for control account managers and project managers.

Activities Performed

The organization routinely holds earned value management system courses. Management is aware of internal earned value management training opportunities and provides opportunities for employees to attend. Management encourages control account manager candidates and project manager candidates to attend these classes to develop a pool of earned value management system–trained personnel. Potential control account managers and project managers are evaluated for their earned value management knowledge. The company retains records of earned value management knowledge assessments.

Verifying Implementation

Records of course attendance and completion are retained. The organization also might maintain a list of potential students so that they can be notified of course offerings. Potential students include those employees likely to be assigned to projects requiring earned value management. A review of control account managers and project managers shows that only those who demonstrate required levels of earned value management knowledge are assigned to earned value management projects.

Process Measurement and Improvement Area

▲ Goal 1: The earned value management measurement processes are planned.

▲ Goal 2: Metrics are collected on the earned value management system processes and periodic reports are produced.

▲ Goal 3: An Earned Value Process Group (EVPG) or similar body is established and meets periodically.

▲ Goal 4: Organizational-level earned value management system process development and improvement activities are planned.

Commitment to Perform

The organization establishes an EVPG and charters it to measure the earned value management process. The organization specifies how frequently the EVPG meets. The organization publishes a formal requirement for periodic collection of earned value management system performance data. The EVPG is formally tasked with providing management periodic reports that include quantitative data about the earned value management system. The measurement process is planned to minimize the impact it has on ongoing projects.

The organization requires that earned value management system improvement activities are planned based on collected earned value management system performance data and that the plans are kept up-to-date. The EVPG must be advised of any changes to processes or policies related to financial, scheduling, organization, or other areas that could impact the earned value management system.

Ability to Perform

The organization provides sufficient resources and authority to the EVPG to allow it to establish measurement points in the earned value management system process. The EVPG allocates these resources to collect earned value management system performance data and to analyze them, produce recommended earned value management system improvements, and create project plans for implementing these improvements. Project managers or functional managers do not impede measurement activities.

The EVPG is notified of changes to the organizational structure, financial systems, project management tools, project management policies and directives, and other systems and procedures that could impact the earned value management system.

Activities Performed

The EVPG staff is formed from personnel who are trained in earned value management and who have experience using earned value management on organization projects. The EVPG members might be project managers, control account managers, schedulers, planners, financial analysts, or others involved in using the earned value management system.

The EVPG meets periodically, as specified by management. The EVPG develops metrics associated with the execution and quality of the earned value management system. The EVPG collects these metrics periodically and analyzes them to determine areas for improvement or disclose earned value management system problems. The EVPG identifies corrective actions and improvements and creates plans for implementing them.

Metrics that might be collected include

- Nominal value of cost accounts

- Work Breakdown Structure (WBS) fan-out

- Control account value versus WBS level

- Number of control accounts per control account manager

- Data latency

- Work package value versus work package duration

- Performance Management Baseline stability

- Value of re-baselines

- Quantity of retroactive adjustments

- Planning package lead time

- Percentage of level-of-effort (LOE) planning

Appendix D presents examples of some of these metrics.

The EVPG reviews all changes to the organization's financial systems, project management tools, project management policies and directives, organizational structure, and other organizational changes that might impact the earned value management system. The EVPG recommends changes to the earned value management system or other systems and procedures so that the earned value management system continues to function effectively.

Verifying Implementation

The EVPG maintains minutes of meetings showing the members present, agenda, topics and points of discussion, decisions reached, and other matters of note. Evidence of periodic data collection exists on all projects using earned value management. Data are collected in a manner that is consistent and that allows the data to be used in analysis to determine project-specific and overall earned value management system improvements. The EVPG prepares reports and forwards them to management with requests for funding and resources needed to execute improvement efforts. The EVPG documents its review of changes to the operating environment (organizational policies, tools, directives, etc.) of the earned value management system and the changes recommended to maintain its performance.

Knowledge Retention Process Area

▲ Goal 1: Through collecting, reviewing, and cataloging project data and experiences, the organization maintains a repository of earned value management information.

Commitment to Perform

The organization publishes a policy requiring the establishment and continuous operation of an earned value management library or other repository of earned value management information. Project managers and team members must contribute project plans, project outcomes, developed tools and techniques, lessons learned, and similar knowledge. The EVPG must contribute its analyses, reports, recommendations, and other items related to the operation of the earned value management system within the organization. The library must possess a retrieval mechanism so that users can locate items of interest.

Ability to Perform

The organization provides resources to collect and retain project-specific earned value management data and other related information that might be of use in future projects. The data is collected with other project data such that analysis of the data can be done in the context of the project from which it was collected. The organization provides resources for centralized retention of earned value management information for past and current projects. The indexing and filing protocols facilitate data retrieval by the workforce, so that the workforce can understand past use of earned value management, lessons learned, and project history.

Activities Performed

The library contains initial project earned value management baselines and final project earned value management outcomes. It also retains earned value management lessons learned and earned value management tools. Library personnel file material in a manner that facilitates its use by others in planning projects, avoiding previous errors, improving baselines, and generally sharing historical experiences. The library also might maintain commercial literature, conference proceedings, and other earned value management–related material. The EVPG periodically reviews the operation of the earned value management library to ensure that retention and filing mechanisms promote the library's use and accessibility.

Verifying Implementation

A location exists for the historical corporate earned value management knowledge. Project staff can easily perform searches of the material and study it for application to current projects or processes. The EVPG contributes to the material and uses it to create earned value management system process improvement plans.

THE EVM³ LEVEL 4 ORGANIZATION

Blue Zephyr was doing well. Could it do better? Senior management started investigating quality and process initiatives associated with International Organization for Standardization (ISO) 9000, lean manufacturing, continuous improvement, and Six Sigma. Howard wondered if Blue Zephyr's ANSI/EIA 748–compliant earned value management system could be improved. He called Heather into his office to discuss the present earned value management system. She said that, in her opinion, a lot of earned value management lessons were being relearned on project after project. She also didn't know how much effort was spent in correcting data errors. She said that there was too much earned value management on-the-job training.

Heather suggested that management fund an earned value management system steering committee to address these concerns. The committee would collect data about the earned value management system and review the overall process for potential areas of improvement. Heather suggested, in addition, that the committee create and run an earned value management training program whereby newly promoted team leaders could become control account managers. She suggested that the committee explore establishing an earned value management library so that team leaders and control account managers could review past project documentation to identify what EVM aspects were done well and what lessons were learned.

Howard agreed and sponsored the creation of an earned value process group (EVPG). Members included some control account managers, project managers, schedulers, cost analysts, and process engineers. At the first meeting, Heather conveyed her views on the EVPG. The EVPG was to do three things: (1) establish a training program and conduct periodic classes, (2) collect data on how well the earned value management system was working, and (3) establish an earned value management library.

Six months later the EVPG presented its first report to Howard and Heather. In it, the EVPG advised that the library was operational and two training sessions had been given to full classrooms. There was a waiting list for entry into the earned value management class. Most students said they wanted to be in the class because those people with knowledge of earned value management were moving up in the company.

The EVPG also reported some surprising news: About 10% of the earned value management data had to be corrected retroactively due to errors in reporting Actual Cost or Earned Value. Detecting and correcting these errors was very time-consuming, and the EVPG felt that the error rate must be reduced. The EVPG also found that most errors went undetected for six weeks; thus, management was receiving erroneous data. The EVPG presented a histogram showing how long bad data went undetected. There was a peak at six weeks and a secondary peak at eight weeks. It also found that one project did not maintain a good earned value management baseline change history and that some approvals were not at the correct level of authority.

The EVPG's report concluded with a list of recommendations to address most of these problem areas and improve the efficiency of using earned value management in Blue Zephyr projects.

▲
CHAPTER 11

EVM³ Level 5: Optimizing Implementation

EVM³ Level 5 represents the highest level of achievement in implementing earned value management. A Level 5 organization puts plans in place, with budgets and champions, to improve the quality and usefulness of earned value management data. Goals are set for improving the earned value management system, such as reducing replans, data latency, and retroactive changes. Metrics track earned value management system improvement projects.

Level 5	• Earned value management system improvement projects • Earned value management system improvement project reporting • Earned value management system quality manager

Level 4	• Earned value management process group • EVMS performance data • Earned value management system training • Earned value management library

Level 3	• ANSI 748 criteria • Material, indirect costs, and subcontractor costs • Control accounts and control account managers • WBS and OBS integrated with cost and scheduling systems

Level 2	• Earned value management data for whole project • CPI and SPI for total project • Direct costs are reported in staff-hours or dollars

Level 1	• No or very limited earned value management • Occasional use at the team level • Frequent re-baselines and poor planning • Limited value

UNDERSTANDING EVM³ LEVEL 5

The EVM³ Level 5 organization recognizes the importance of continuously improving its earned value management system. Through the Earned Value Process Group (EVPG) and support from senior management, the earned value management system process is made more accurate in measuring project cost and schedule. The earned value management system becomes more standardized, less costly, and more responsive to management needs. Data are available more quickly for decision-making. A formal long-term plan for incorporating new tools and techniques is established and tracked.

KEY PROCESS AREAS

Defect Prevention

▲ Goal 1: Defect prevention activities are planned.

▲ Goal 2: Common causes of defects are sought out and identified.

▲ Goal 3: Common causes of defects are prioritized and systematically eliminated.

Commitment to Perform
The organization establishes the position of earned value management quality manager (although the title may be slightly different). This person oversees the review of project planning, project processes, financial and scheduling systems, the earned value management system, and project personnel to reveal any weaknesses that could introduce defective data into the earned value management system. The earned value management quality manager reports systemic weaknesses to management and prioritizes the weaknesses for reduction or elimination.

Ability to Perform

The organization assigns and funds the position of earned value management quality manager. This person has sufficient resources to provide earned value management system defect prevention services to both the organization and individual projects in the planning, execution, and control process phases.

The organization keeps the quality manager aware of projects undergoing initial planning or replanning, phase or gate review, and other critical events that could establish a new baseline. The quality manager is aware of changes to the earned value management system, the rationale for these changes, and which team members are implementing these changes.

The earned value management system quality manager also receives project reports showing changes to baselines, corrections of errors, resubmissions of reports and variance analyses, and other information related to the correction of earned value management system errors or omissions. The quality manager has the skills and tools to identify root causes of errors by performing statistical or other rigorous analysis of the earned value management system and data.

The organization provides funds to eliminate earned value management system defects.

The quality manager coordinates activities with the EVPG.

Activities Performed

The quality manager reviews each project's use of the earned value management system implementation as it completes planning or replanning. The quality manager identifies any errors or omissions in implementing earned value management that could result in earned value management data errors or loss of accuracy. The quality manager also makes recommendations to increase the accuracy of the project's ERM data. Projects correct any errors in application of earned value management.

If inadequate training is the source of error, the quality manager advises the EVPG to revise the earned value management system training program.

The quality manager reviews all planned changes to the earned value management system for the potential introduction of errors and assists in developing a testing plan to show that the changes have yielded the desired outcome. The quality manager also reviews regression testing plans to see that they adequately test for any loss of previous capability or accuracy in earned value management data.

The earned value management system quality manager performs analysis on earned value management errors or omissions that are revealed through frequent re-baselines, rejections of reports or variance analyses, or data corrections. This analysis identifies root causes and suggests corrective action.

Corrective actions are undertaken to reduce earned value management system errors or to improve the efficiency of the overall earned value management system.

The quality manager works with the EVPG or is a member of the EVPG. The quality manager recommends earned value management system improvement projects from the recommendations of the EVPG. Changes to the earned value management processes are tracked and the effectiveness of these changes in reducing defects is reported.

Verifying Implementation
The organization documents the person assigned as the earned value management system quality manager and identifies the reporting relationships of this individual.

The earned value management system quality manager maintains evidence of having reviewed a project's earned value management system implementation. When a project's earned value management implementation must be changed, these changes are documented to determine if a shared root cause exists for commonly occurring errors.

The quality manager documents and approves changes to the earned value management system. In addition, the quality manager retains test plans and results of changes to the earned value management system.

The quality manager prepares reports that provide statistical or other evidence of any systemic errors detected as a result of analysis of earned value management corrections and revisions. The quality manager reviews recommendations made by the EVPG and selects those for implementation within EVM improvement budgets and priorities. The quality manager retains a history of changes to the earned value management system along with any resulting changes to the accuracy and effectiveness of the earned value management system.

Improvement Process Area

▲ Goal 1: Continuous process improvement is planned.

▲ Goal 2: Participation in the organization's earned value management process improvement activities is organization-wide.

Commitment to Perform

The organization requires an earned value management system process improvement plan that consists of tools, processes, training systems, and policies and/or other improvement activities. The organization establishes a timeline for implementation of improvement activities.

Ability to Perform

The organization provides resources for the development of an earned value management system process improvement plan. The plan is funded, assigned a project manager, and managed as a project. The timeline for the scheduled changes and improvements to the earned value management system is consistent with the resources allocated.

Activities Performed

The organization has an active process for soliciting earned value management system improvements. The organization selects earned value management system improvement projects and funds them based on candidate improvement projects recommended by the EVPG or others in the organization. The organization plans and funds these efforts and manages them as formal projects. The organization applies earned value management to earned value management system improvement projects. It evaluates project outcomes against project goals.

Verifying Implementation

The organization maintains a list of recommended earned value management system improvements. These recommendations include suggestions from the EVPG and organization staff. Based on funding and objectives, at least one earned value management system improvement project is underway. Periodic reports track project status. The organization records the results of completed improvement projects to show how each project performed in terms of cost, schedule, and objectives in meeting its goals.

THE EVM³ LEVEL 5 ORGANIZATION

Howard and Heather continued to get reports from the EVPG about the company's ANSI/EIA 748–compliant earned value management system. The reports identified trends in the accuracy and timeliness of the earned value management data. The reports included data detailing how well project managers and control account managers were doing in performing correct analyses of data and taking appropriate management actions. Blue Zephyr's continued focus on earned value management made its culture one in which earned value management terms were commonly used in most project discussions.

Heather asked the EVPG to create a project charter for improving the earned value management system. Howard approved the charter and provided funding for the earned value management system improvement project. The EVPG developed its project plan and presented it to Howard and Heather. Both thought the plan was sound and told the EVPG to proceed. The EVPG reported status on the earned value management improvement project using earned value management data.

The earned value management improvement project ended eight months later. A year later, retroactive corrections to the earned value management data had been reduced from 10% to 3%. Also, error detection time went from six weeks to three, with corrections being made within one week of detection. The project also established a simpler means for reviewing and approving baseline changes. All projects were using the new process and keeping good baseline change control and records.

Meanwhile, the corporate board of directors saw the value and size of the company increase as profits rose and customers increased. As company profit was based on successful projects and satisfied customers, the board created a new board position: Chief Project Officer (CPO). Heather was named the new CPO. Her efforts had transformed Blue Zephyr from a struggling business into a successful corporation.

Back in the Program Management Office (PMO), a few legacy projects still were not using earned value management. These projects were the exception and would soon end.

Robert found himself excluded from most management meetings and decided to retire. Carol, without the political support of her former boss, was let go.

At Heather's first board meeting, members expressed concern about the reporting requirements mandated by the Sarbanes-Oxley Act. This act requires the CFO and the CEO to attest to the accuracy of a corporation's forward-looking financial statements. Most of Blue Zephyr's expenses were for project staff; most of its profits came from completed projects. The board was wrestling with how to make accurate forecasts of project expenses, revenues, and profits. Heather spoke up, "I think we can make the CFO and CEO comfortable with the company's financial forecasts. We can use a project cost and schedule control method that can accurately estimate when our projects will complete and how much our projects will cost."

CLOSING REMARKS ON HEATHER, BLUE ZEPHYR, AND EARNED VALUE MANAGEMENT

While Heather and her career progression with Blue Zephyr is fiction, earned value management is becoming more important as one of today's essential project management tools. Within the U.S. government and its contractors, the ability to perform earned value management is essential to securing budgets and winning contracts. Within industry at large and worldwide, more and more organizations are seeing earned value management as part of project and portfolio management. Some have made the connection between earned value management data analysis and corporate forward-looking financial forecasts (Sarbanes-Oxley). The author expects that Heather's fictional career progression will be played out within real project organizations, sporadically at first, and then with increasing frequency. Project-focused organizations will see the value of employees who can apply earned value management to even the smallest projects and also help the organization attain higher levels of earned value management system maturity.

The author has worked with several clients whose interest in EVM was internal, not imposed by regulation or contract. EVM was implemented in a few days because good schedules and good budgets were in place. These are key elements of an earned value management system. The EVM³ Level 2 capability is sufficient for these clients' needs and places them in a good position for Level 3. Other organizations that have attained EVM³ Level 3 can look toward Level 4 and Level 5 to reduce the cost of operating their EVMS while adding accuracy and timeliness to the data.

Recall that, like all cultural and systemic changes, earned value management will take time to implement. Hopefully your use of the EVM³ maturity model will shorten this time, since not all ANSI/EIA 748 guidelines need to be met at once, or perhaps at all. Make sure you have good data. Good data will show the value of EVM. Bad data (usually overstated Earned Value) will lead to false earned value management analysis, and the abandonment of earned value management for not accurately reporting project cost and schedule information. To abandon earned value management would be to abandon one of the most power project management tools available. Focus on a good plan (Planned Value) and accurate Earned Value.

I hope you have found this book useful in understanding earned value management and how you might be able to implement or improve your earned value management system.

▲

Appendices

Common Earned Value Management Work-in-Process Measurement Methods

Table A-1 lists the most common earned value management work-in-process (WIP) measures, also sometimes called earned value techniques (EVTs). Neither American National Standards Institute (ANSI/EIA) 748 nor the Earned Value Management Maturity Model (EVM³) discusses WIPs. An organization must select the measurement methods it will use to obtain an estimate of Earned Value for partially completed work and assign an accurate Earned Value. One method will rarely apply to a whole project, as some work packages have a short duration and others have a long one, and some projects have definitive, known products and others have very intangible products.

Table A-1 lists WIPs from most to least desirable in terms of the accuracy and objectiveness of the WIP. The list is not inclusive, and organizations are free to create any meaningful measurement scheme.

Table A-1. Work-in-Process Measures

Earned Value Technique	Description	Remarks
Percentage of Units Complete	The Earned Value is a percentage of the Planned Value based on a count of the number of units completed divided by a fixed amount of units to be produced.	When it is possible to count completed units out of a total number to be completed, this method provides the most accurate Earned Value. It is suitable for any activity duration.
Estimated Percentage of Units Complete	The Earned Value is an estimated percentage of the Planned Value based on a count of the number of units completed divided by an expected number of units to be produced.	This technique provides more flexibility than Percentage of Units Complete and can be used when the final quantity is estimated, but not known exactly (for example, if the product is lines of code or function points).
Estimated Percentage Complete	The Earned Value is an estimated percentage of the Planned Value based on the control account manager's experience with similar tasks.	This WIP can be used for activities over two reporting periods, but runs the risk of overestimating the work completed or underestimating the total scope of work, leading to activities whose Estimated Percentage Complete asymptotically approaches 100%.
Fixed Formula	This WIP gives Earned Value as a fixed percentage of Planned Value for starting and ending a task. Examples include 0%/100%, 50%/50%, 30%/70%, etc.	This method work wells only for activities spanning one or two reporting periods. Once a task is started, no Earned Value can be credited for work under way but not completed.
Weighted Milestones	This technique assigns a fixed amount of the Planned Value to two or more milestones within the activity or work package.	This method works well if a milestone can be defined for each reporting period, but can become hard to track if some milestones slip into other periods. Breaking down the milestones into individual work packages and applying the Fixed Formula to each is preferred.

Table A-1. Work-in-Process Measures (continued)

Earned Value Technique	Description	Remarks
Apportioned Effort	This WIP allows one work package to obtain Earned Value based on the progress of a related work package.	This method may be applied to tasks that are paced by the work completed in other tasks. It is seldom used and requires administrative effort.
Level of Effort (LOE)	This method is for activities that do not produce any product (for example, project services such as operating a laboratory, configuration management, etc.).	LOE biases the total project's Earned Value data toward an on-schedule condition and can hide significant schedule variances. It should be avoided wherever possible.

▲

APPENDIX B

EVM³ Level and U.S. Office of Management and Budget Scoring Rules

Table B-1 associates the Earned Value Management Maturity Model (EVM³) levels with the U.S. Office of Management and Budget (OMB) previously used (through FY 2007) scoring method for earned value management in addition to the organization's earned value management system maturity, OMB scoring also relied on project performance (where cost and schedule are measured using earned value management).

Table B-1. Relationship of EVM³ Level to OMB Scoring used through FY 2007

EVM³ Level	OMB Score	OMB Expectation
1	1–2	1. There is no evidence of a performance baseline. 2. Agency seems to re-baseline rather than report variances.
2	3–4	3. Agency uses required earned value management system, but the process within the agency is new and not fully implemented, or there are weaknesses for this individual project's earned value management system information. 4. Agency uses earned value management system and is within the variance levels for two of the three criteria, but it needs to work on the third issue.

Table B-1. Relationship of EVM^3 Level to OMB Score (continued)

EVM^3 Level	OMB Score	OMB Expectation
3	5	5. Agency will use, or uses, an earned value management system that meets American National Standards Institute 748 and project is earning the value as planned for cost, schedule, and performance goals.
4	N/A	N/A
5	N/A	N/A

As of this book's publication date, OMB had only said that a numerical scoring methodology will no longer be used in evaluating earned value management. A conversation with an OMB evaluator suggested that a ranking of earned value management would still be performed even if no formal scoring system was used. The author believes that this ranking will follow closely the previous scoring. Readers whose responsibilities include program review by OMB are cautioned to contact OMB directly for the latest policy on earned value management evaluation.

ANSI/EIA 748 Guidelines (Unabridged)

Organization

a) Define the authorized work elements for the program. A work breakdown structure (WBS), tailored for effective internal management control, is commonly used in this process.

b) Identify the program organizational structure including the major subcontractors responsible for accomplishing the authorized work, and define the organizational elements in which work will be planned and controlled.

c) Provide for the integration of the company's planning, scheduling, budgeting, work authorization and cost accumulation processes with each other, and as appropriate, the program work breakdown structure and the program organizational structure.

d) Identify the company organization or function responsible for controlling overhead (indirect costs).

e) Provide for integration of the program work breakdown structure and the program organizational structure in a manner that permits cost and schedule performance measurement by elements of either or both structures as needed.

Planning, Scheduling, and Budgeting

a) Schedule the authorized work in a manner which describes the sequence of work and identifies significant task interdependencies required to meet the requirements of the program.

b) Identify physical products, milestones, technical performance goals, or other indicators that will be used to measure progress.

c) Establish and maintain a time-phased budget baseline, at the control account level, against which program performance can be measured. Initial budgets established for performance measurement will be based on either internal management goals or the external customer negotiated target cost including estimates for authorized but undefinitized work. Budget for far-term efforts may be held in higher-level accounts until an appropriate time for allocation at the control account level. On government contracts, if an over target baseline is used for performance measurement reporting purposes, prior notification must be provided to the customer.

d) Establish budgets for authorized work with identification of significant cost elements (labor, material, etc.) as needed for internal management and for control of subcontractors.

e) To the extent it is practical to identify the authorized work in discrete work packages, establish budgets for this work in terms of dollars, hours, or other measurable units. Where the entire control account is not subdivided into work packages, identify the far term effort in larger planning packages for budget and scheduling purposes.

f) Provide that the sum of all work package budgets plus planning package budgets within a control account equals the control account budget.

g) Identify and control level of effort activity by time-phased budgets established for this purpose. Only that effort which is unmeasurable or for which measurement is impractical may be classified as level of effort.

h) Establish overhead budgets for each significant organizational component of the company for expenses, which will become indirect costs. Reflect in the program budgets, at the appropriate level, the amounts in overhead pools that are planned to be allocated to the program as indirect costs.

i) Identify management reserves and undistributed budget.

j) Provide that the program target cost goal is reconciled with the sum of all internal program budgets and management reserves.

Accounting

a) Record direct costs in a manner consistent with the budgets in a formal system controlled by the general books of account.

b) When a work breakdown structure is used, summarize direct costs from control accounts into the work breakdown structure without allocation of a single control account to two or more work breakdown structure elements.

c) Summarize direct costs from the control accounts into the contractor's organizational elements without allocation of a single control account to two or more organizational elements.

d) Record all indirect costs which will be allocated to the contract.

e) Identify unit costs, equivalent units costs, or lot costs when needed.

f) For EVMS, the material accounting system will provide for:

(1) Accurate cost accumulation and assignment of costs to control accounts in a manner consistent with the budgets using recognized, acceptable, costing techniques.

(2) Cost performance measurement at the point in time most suitable for the category of material involved, but no earlier than the time of progress payments or actual receipt of material.

(3) Full accountability of all material purchased for the program including the residual inventory.

Analysis and Management

a) At least on a monthly basis, generate the following information at the control account and other levels as necessary for management control using actual cost data from, or reconcilable with, the accounting system:

(1) Comparison of the amount of planned budget and the amount of budget earned for work accomplished. This comparison provides the schedule variance.

(2) Comparison of the amount of the budget earned the actual (applied where appropriate) direct costs for the same work. This comparison provides the cost variance.

b) Identify, at least monthly, the significant differences between both planned and actual schedule performance and planned and actual cost performance, and provide the reasons for the variances in the detail needed by program management.

c) Identify budgeted and applied (or actual) indirect costs at the level and frequency needed by management for effective control, along with the reasons for any significant variances.

d) Summarize the data elements and associated variances through the program organization and/or work breakdown structure to support management needs and any customer reporting specified in the contract.

e) Implement managerial actions taken as the result of earned value information.

f) Develop revised estimates of cost at completion based on performance to date, commitment values for material, and estimates of future conditions. Compare this information with the performance measurement baseline to identify variances at completion important to company management and any applicable customer reporting requirements including statements of funding requirements.

Revisions and Data Management

a) Incorporate authorized changes in a timely manner, recording the effects of such changes in budgets and schedules. In the directed effort prior to negotiation of a change, base such revisions on the amount estimated and budgeted to the program organizations.

b) Reconcile current budgets to prior budgets in terms of changes to the authorized work and internal replanning in the detail needed by management for effective control.

c) Control retroactive changes to records pertaining to work performed that would change previously reported amounts for actual costs, earned value, or budgets. Adjustments should be made only for correction of errors, routine accounting adjustments, effects of customer or management directed changes, or to improve the baseline integrity and accuracy of performance measurement data.

d) Prevent revisions to the program budget except for authorized changes.

e) Document changes to the performance measurement baseline.

▲
APPENDIX D

Concepts of Earned Value Management System Metrics

EVM³ Level 4 requires that earned value management system metrics are collected about the operation of the earned value management system. No specific metrics are required. The organization should choose its metrics with the goals of learning how well the earned value management system operates and improving the system. The following examples are meant to stimulate discussion about what metrics might be useful.

NUMBER OF CONTROL ACCOUNTS BY PROJECT BUDGET

Plotting the value of work packages versus the number of work packages gives an indication of whether the data will be too summarized for effective management or so detailed as to burden the organization with administrative load. This plot could be drawn for (1) all the work packages in a program or (2) throughout an organization to indicate projects that are typical for the organization and those that are not. Figures D-1 and D-2 illustrate two ways to plot number of control accounts by project budget.

In Figure D-1, the number of control accounts is plotted on the x-axis. A project with a small budget can make do with less control accounts; as the budget increases, more accounts are needed.

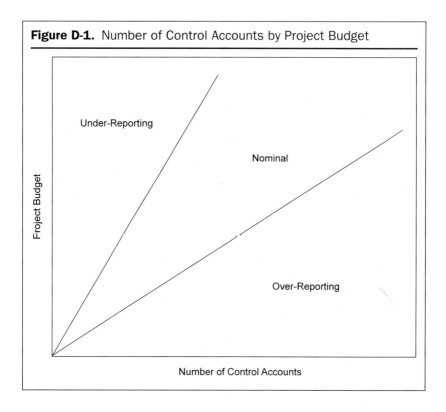

Figure D-1. Number of Control Accounts by Project Budget

WORK BREAKDOWN STRUCTURE FAN-OUT RATIO

The Work Breakdown Structure (WBS) fan-out ratio reflects the number of WBS elements spawned from the next-higher WBS element. For example, the first level of the WBS could spawn as many as 10 or more second-level WBS elements (a WBS ratio of 10:1). At lower levels of the WBS, reducing the number of WBS offspring is desirable. Fewer offspring means less administrative burden during the periodic accounting of Earned Value data. Reducing the WBS fan-out ratio at lower levels also reduces the tendency to over-manage smaller tasks.

Consideration of maintaining accountability to one organizational element must still be considered in defining WBS ele-

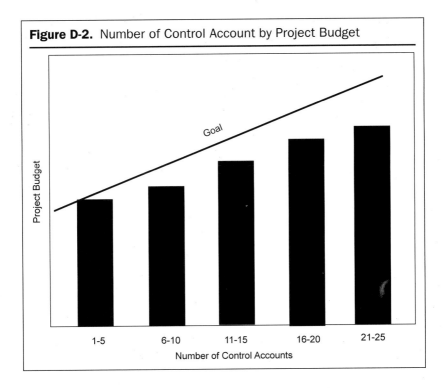

Figure D-2. Number of Control Account by Project Budget

ments. However, the ability to associate a control account with one OBS and WBS element and the requirement to be able to collect cost data for just this element are always the primary considerations. This chart can show typical project structures but should not be used to define or limit them.

VALUE PER WBS LEVEL

Plotting the value of each WBS element shows whether any WBS elements stand out as atypical. Excessively high values mean the WBS is candidate for splitting into two WBS elements at that level; low values mean the WBS is a candidate for being combined with another WBS element, provided accountability for the work is still within one organizational element.

Figure D-3. WBS Fan-Out Ratio

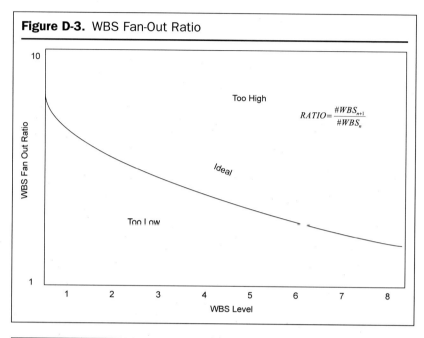

Figure D-4. Value per WBS Level

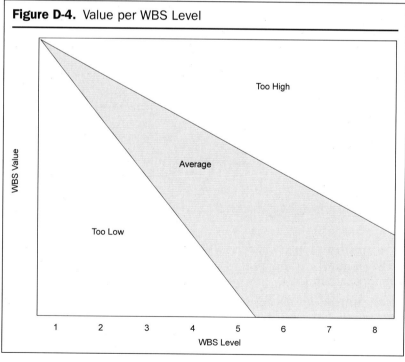

However, as with the previous example (D-3), the ability to associate a Control Account with one OBS and WBS element and the requirement to be able to collect cost data for just this element are always the primary considerations.

CONTROL ACCOUNT MANAGER WORKLOAD

Overloaded control account managers (CAMs) cannot provide effective management and maintain up-to-date earned value management data. A plot of the project's or organization's number of open work packages versus the number of trained CAMs shows if any data points fall out of the norm. This finding can alert management to define fewer and higher-level work packages, or train more CAMs to handle the earned value management workload.

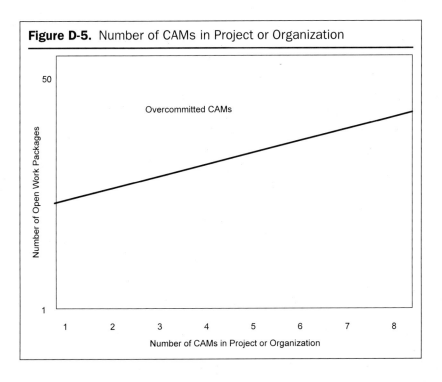

Figure D-5. Number of CAMs in Project or Organization

CAMs and organizations can be assigned multiple control accounts as long as only one OBS element manages the control account. This can cause excessive CAM workload if there are too few training CAMs or they are assigned to too many projects. Earned value management planning and data accuracy is likely to suffer.

EARNED VALUE MANAGEMENT DATA LATENCY

Plotting data latency shows how quickly the various project accounting systems can provide the CAM with earned value management data so that analysis can occur. It also can show how long it takes to complete the earned value management reports once the data are available. These indicators can point to systemic problems in getting the financial data and assessing the status of work, as well as demonstrate CAM workforce

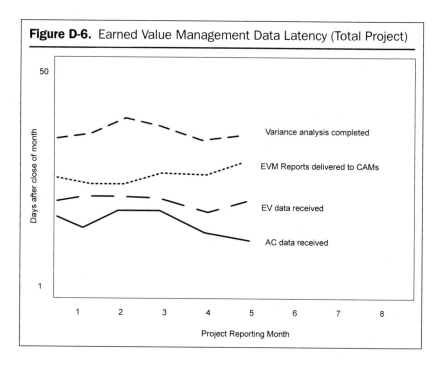

Figure D-6. Earned Value Management Data Latency (Total Project)

overload. In addition, this plot can point to a symptom of "Set the Earned Value equal to the Actual Cost" for "estimated" Earned Value values should the Actual Cost latency be less than the Earned Value latency.

WORK PACKAGE VALUE VERSUS WORK PACKAGE DURATION

Plotting work package value versus work package duration shows if large but short-term work packages exist in the project or organization. These packages might be candidates for breaking into several smaller work packages to provide better visibility and accuracy for the short duration of these tasks. The value of the work package is plotted over the work package duration. This could also be done at the control account level.

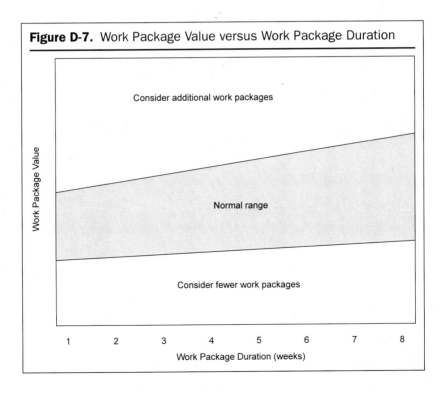

Figure D-7. Work Package Value versus Work Package Duration

NUMBER OF REPLANS OR BASELINE CHANGES

Plotting the number of replans during various periods or time shows the volatility of the project or organization's baseline. Replans due to planning packages might be shown as a reasonable lower limit.

It is important to label external events that may cause replanning, like annual funding changes, so that these events are excluded from internal replanning efforts. Also some replanning early in the project may reflect knowledge gains as the project team gets into the real work. Therefore some peaks within the first few months of a project might not be cause for alarm.

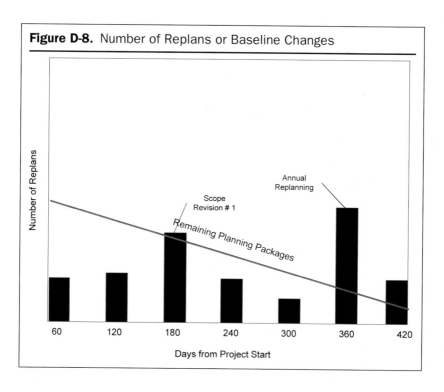

Figure D-8. Number of Replans or Baseline Changes

NUMBER AND TYPE OF RETROACTIVE ADJUSTMENTS

By plotting the quantity of retroactive adjustments by the delay in the adjustment, it is possible to determine both the degree of accounting errors and the time required to locate and correct them. This example shows retroactive changes to both Earned Value and Actual Cost separately so that focus can be applied to the most troublesome metric.

VALUE OF REPLANS AS A PERCENTAGE OF BUDGET AT COMPLETE

Plotting the value of replans as a histogram shows how extensive each replan was to the project or organization. Note that *percentage of total program* value is used versus *actual value*. This value uses data relative to the program size and permits comparison between different programs and organizations.

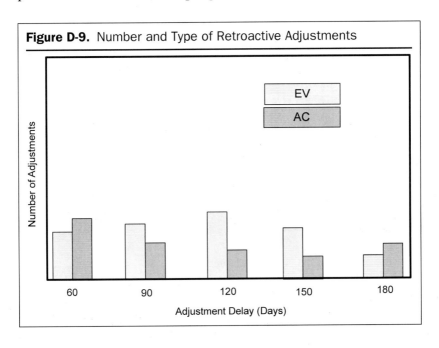

Figure D-9. Number and Type of Retroactive Adjustments

It is important to know how significant a replan is to the project baseline. Frequent small internal replans may be part of adjustments to keep the original project plan current with evolving knowledge. Some large replans can be for external changes, which must be accommodated. However, large replans can be disruptive to ongoing efforts and can also be due to an unwillingness to change a bad plan until late in the project.

PLANNING PACKAGE LEAD TIME

Planning packages should be converted to work packages once the needed detail is available. They should not be left for the

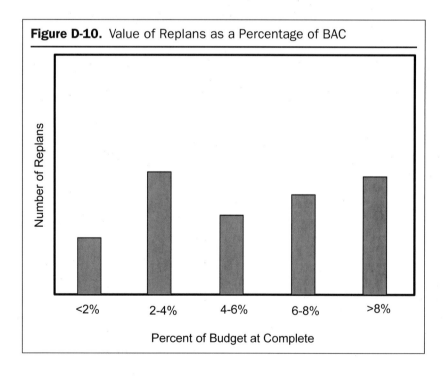

Figure D-10. Value of Replans as a Percentage of BAC

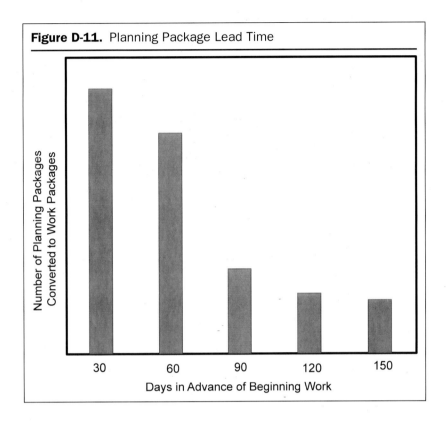

Figure D-11. Planning Package Lead Time

last moment. A histogram of planning package lead time shows how proactive an organization or project is in detail planning future work packages.

PERCENTAGE OF LEVEL OF EFFORT AND ESTIMATED PERCENTAGE COMPLETE WORK PACKAGES BY PROJECT

For each project or organization, a plot of the percentage of tasks measured as level of effort (LOE) or "CAM's estimate" will give a relative measure of the "accuracy" of the Earned Value (Figure D-12). Lower percentages are desired. Note that the only activities plotted are ones with an Earned Value that is a "guess" or ones that cannot have schedule variance.

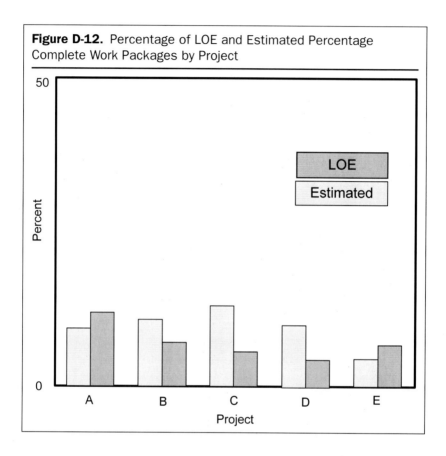

Figure D-12. Percentage of LOE and Estimated Percentage Complete Work Packages by Project

Qualitative assessment of Earned Value is always better than estimates or level of effort. This chart allows comparison of various projects, perhaps in a portfolio, use of estimating or LOE techniques. Comparisons and lessons learned should be drawn from the data so that generally the organization moves toward more quantitative assessment of Earned Value.

Index